Autodesk® Vault Professional 2018 Data Management for Autodesk® Inventor® Users

Student Guide
1ˢᵗ Edition

Authorized Publisher

ASCENT - Center for Technical Knowledge®
Autodesk® Vault Professional 2018
Data Management for Autodesk® Inventor® Users
1st Edition

Prepared and produced by:

ASCENT Center for Technical Knowledge
630 Peter Jefferson Parkway, Suite 175
Charlottesville, VA 22911

866-527-2368
www.ASCENTed.com

Lead Contributor: Barb Nash

ASCENT - Center for Technical Knowledge is a division of Rand Worldwide, Inc., providing custom developed knowledge products and services for leading engineering software applications. ASCENT is focused on specializing in the creation of education programs that incorporate the best of classroom learning and technology-based training offerings.

We welcome any comments you may have regarding this student guide, or any of our products. To contact us please email: feedback@ASCENTed.com.

The following are registered trademarks or trademarks of Autodesk, Inc., and/or its subsidiaries and/or affiliates in the USA and other countries: 123D, 3ds Max, Alias, ATC, AutoCAD LT, AutoCAD, Autodesk, the Autodesk logo, Autodesk 123D, Autodesk Homestyler, Autodesk Inventor, Autodesk MapGuide, Autodesk Streamline, AutoLISP, AutoSketch, AutoSnap, AutoTrack, Backburner, Backdraft, Beast BIM 360, Burn, Buzzsaw, CADmep, CAiCE, CAMduct, Civil 3D, Combustion, Communication Specification, Configurator 360, Constructware, Content Explorer, Creative Bridge, Dancing Baby (image), DesignCenter, DesignKids, DesignStudio, Discreet, DWF, DWG, DWG (design/logo), DWG Extreme, DWG TrueConvert, DWG TrueView, DWGX, DXF, Ecotect, Ember, ESTmep, FABmep, Face Robot, FBX, Fempro, Fire, Flame, Flare, Flint, ForceEffect, FormIt 360, Freewheel, Fusion 360, Glue, Green Building Studio, Heidi, Homestyler, HumanIK, i-drop, ImageModeler, Incinerator, Inferno, InfraWorks, Instructables, Instructables (stylized robot design/logo), Inventor, Inventor HSM, Inventor LT, Lustre, Maya, Maya LT, MIMI, Mockup 360, Moldflow Plastics Advisers, Moldflow Plastics Insight, Moldflow, Moondust, MotionBuilder, Movimento, MPA (design/logo), MPA, MPI (design/logo), MPX (design/logo), MPX, Mudbox, Navisworks, ObjectARX, ObjectDBX, Opticore, P9, Pier 9, Pixlr, Pixlr-o-matic, Productstream, Publisher 360, RasterDWG, RealDWG, ReCap, ReCap 360, Remote, Revit LT, Revit, RiverCAD, Robot, Scaleform, Showcase, Showcase 360, SketchBook, Smoke, Socialcam, Softimage, Spark & Design, Spark Logo, Sparks, SteeringWheels, Stitcher, Stone, StormNET, TinkerBox, Tinkercad, Tinkerplay, ToolClip, Topobase, Toxik, TrustedDWG, T-Splines, ViewCube, Visual LISP, Visual, VRED, Wire, Wiretap, WiretapCentral, XSI.

NASTRAN is a registered trademark of the National Aeronautics Space Administration.

All other brand names, product names, or trademarks belong to their respective holders.

General Disclaimer:

Notwithstanding any language to the contrary, nothing contained herein constitutes nor is intended to constitute an offer, inducement, promise, or contract of any kind. The data contained herein is for informational purposes only and is not represented to be error free. ASCENT, its agents and employees, expressly disclaim any liability for any damages, losses or other expenses arising in connection with the use of its materials or in connection with any failure of performance, error, omission even if ASCENT, or its representatives, are advised of the possibility of such damages, losses or other expenses. No consequential damages can be sought against ASCENT or Rand Worldwide, Inc. for the use of these materials by any third parties or for any direct or indirect result of that use.

The information contained herein is intended to be of general interest to you and is provided "as is", and it does not address the circumstances of any particular individual or entity. Nothing herein constitutes professional advice, nor does it constitute a comprehensive or complete statement of the issues discussed thereto. ASCENT does not warrant that the document or information will be error free or will meet any particular criteria of performance or quality. In particular (but without limitation) information may be rendered inaccurate by changes made to the subject of the materials (i.e. applicable software). Rand Worldwide, Inc. specifically disclaims any warranty, either expressed or implied, including the warranty of fitness for a particular purpose.

AS-VLT1801-DMI1NU-SG   //   IS-VLT1801-DMI1NU-SG

Contents

Preface

*Autodesk® Vault Professional 2018: Data Management for Autodesk® Inventor®
Users* introduces the Autodesk Vault Professional 2018 software to Autodesk
Inventor Users. This student guide is intended for Autodesk Inventor users who
need to access their design files from the Autodesk Vault software. It provides an
introduction to the Autodesk Vault Professional software and focuses on Autodesk
Vault's features for managing design projects with the Autodesk Inventor software
from a user's perspective.

Students can use the Autodesk Vault Professional 2018 software and should use
the Autodesk Inventor 2018 software to complete the exercises in this student
guide. Note that this student guide does not cover administrative functionality.
Hands-on exercises are included to reinforce how to manage the design workflow
process using the Autodesk Vault Professional software. Included with this
student guide is a training Vault that can be used alongside a production Vault, to
ensure that both Vaults can be accessed from the Autodesk Vault software.

Topics Covered

- Introduction to Autodesk Vault Features

- Using the Autodesk Vault client

- Searching the Vault

- Working with non-CAD Files in the Vault

- Working with Inventor Files in the Vault

- Customizing the User Interface

- Data Management and Reusing Design Data

- Items and Bill of Materials

- Change Management

Note on Software Setup

This student guide assumes a standard installation of the software using the default preferences during installation. Lectures and practices use the standard software templates and default options for the Content Libraries.

Students and Educators can Access Free Autodesk Software and Resources

Autodesk challenges you to get started with free educational licenses for professional software and creativity apps used by millions of architects, engineers, designers, and hobbyists today. Bring Autodesk software into your classroom, studio, or workshop to learn, teach, and explore real-world design challenges the way professionals do.

Get started today - register at the Autodesk Education Community and download one of the many Autodesk software applications available.

Visit www.autodesk.com/joinedu/

Note: Free products are subject to the terms and conditions of the end-user license and services agreement that accompanies the software. The software is for personal use for education purposes and is not intended for classroom or lab use.

Lead Contributor: Barb Nash

With extensive experience in project management and eLearning development, Barb's primary responsibilities include the design, development, and project management of courseware for Product Lifecycle Management (PLM) products such as Autodesk Vault and Autodesk Fusion Lifecycle. Her work also involves the development of custom training that is designed and configured to a company's specific environment, processes, and roles.

Prior to joining ASCENT in 2005, Barb managed a technical support team for 10 years supporting CAD and PDM/PLM software.

Barb is a Professional Engineer and holds a degree in Aerospace Engineering. She is also a certified Project Management Professional (PMP) and trained in Instructional Design.

Barb Nash has been the Lead Contributor for *Autodesk Vault Professional: Data Management for Autodesk Inventor Users* since its initial release in 2013.

In this Guide

The following images highlight some of the features that can be found in this Student Guide.

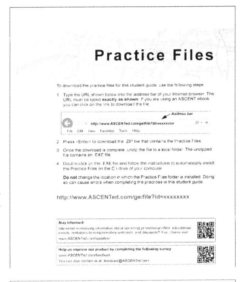

Practice Files

The Practice Files page tells you how to download and install the practice files that are provided with this student guide.

FTP link for practice files

Chapters

Each chapter begins with a brief introduction and a list of the chapter's Learning Objectives.

Learning Objectives for the chapter

Side notes

Side notes are hints or additional information for the current topic.

Instructional Content

Each chapter is split into a series of sections of instructional content on specific topics. These lectures include the descriptions, step-by-step procedures, figures, hints, and information you need to achieve the chapter's Learning Objectives.

Practice Objectives

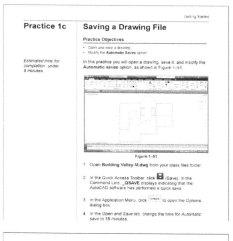

Practices

Practices enable you to use the software to perform a hands-on review of a topic.

Some practices require you to use prepared practice files, which can be downloaded from the link found on the Practice Files page.

Chapter Review Questions

Chapter review questions, located at the end of each chapter, enable you to review the key concepts and learning objectives of the chapter.

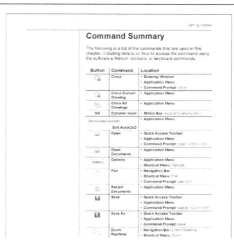

Command Summary

The Command Summary is located at the end of each chapter. It contains a list of the software commands that are used throughout the chapter, and provides information on where the command is found in the software.

Practice Files

To download the practice files for this student guide, use the following steps:

1. Type the URL shown below into the address bar of your Internet browser. The URL must be typed **exactly as shown**. If you are using an ASCENT ebook, you can click on the link to download the file.

Address bar

http://www.ASCENTed.com/getfile?id=tetraoninae

File   Edit   View   Favorites   Tools   Help

2. Press <Enter> to download the .ZIP file that contains the Practice Files.

3. Once the download is complete, unzip the file to a local folder. The unzipped file contains an .EXE file.

4. Double-click on the .EXE file and follow the instructions to automatically install the Practice Files on the C:\ drive of your computer.

   Do not change the location in which the Practice Files folder is installed. Doing so can cause errors when completing the practices in this student guide.

5. Move **Vault_Training.mdf** and **Vault_Training_log.LDF** to the *C:\Program Files(86)\Microsoft SQL Server\MSSQL11.AUTODESKVAULT\ MSSQL\DATA* or *C:\Program Files\Microsoft SQL Server\MSSQL11.AUTODESKVAULT\ MSSQL\DATA folder.*

http://www.ASCENTed.com/getfile?id=tetraoninae

Stay Informed!

Interested in receiving information about upcoming promotional offers, educational events, invitations to complimentary webcasts, and discounts? If so, please visit:

www.ASCENTed.com/updates/

Help us improve our product by completing the following survey:

www.ASCENTed.com/feedback

You can also contact us at: *feedback@ASCENTed.com*

Software Setup

Attach the Database

1. From the Start menu, select **Autodesk>Autodesk Data Management> Autodesk Data Management Server Console 2018**.

2. Log in as **Administrator** without a password.

3. Select **Vaults**, as shown below.

4. Select **Actions>Attach>***Advanced* tab to attach the Vault. Fill in the following details, as follows:

   1. **Data File**: *C:\Program Files(86)\Microsoft SQL Server\MSSQL 11. AUTODESKVAULT\MSSQL\DATA\Vault_Training.mdf*
      or
      C:\Program Files\Microsoft SQL Server\MSSQL11.AUTODESKVAULT\ MSSQL\DATA\Vault_Training.mdf

   2. **Log File**: Filled in automatically

   3. **File Store**: *C:\Vault Data Management Practice Files\Vault Training*

   4. **Vault Name**: Filled in automatically

5. Click **OK**. The Attach Progress dialog box opens.

6. In the Autodesk Data Management Server Console dialog box, click **OK** when prompted that the vault was attached successfully.

7. Select the **Vault_Training** vault.

8. Select **Actions>Content Indexing Service**.

9. In the Content Indexing Service dialog box, select **Yes, enable the Content Indexing Service**.

---

10. Click **OK**.

11. In the Autodesk Data Management Server Console dialog box, click **OK**. Remain in the Autodesk Data Management Server Console to create users.

Set Up Users

1. If the Autodesk Data Management Server Console is open, skip to step 3. If not, from the Start menu, select **Autodesk>Autodesk Data Management> Autodesk Data Management Server Console 2018** and log in as Administrator. No password is required.

2. Select **Tools>Administration** and select the *Security* tab.

3. Click **Users...**.

4. Click **New User**.

5. Set the *First Name* to **user1**.

6. Set the *User Name* to **user1**. Do not enter a password.

7. Click **Roles...** and select **Administrator, Document Editor (Level 2), Change Order Editor (Level 2), and Item Editor (Level 2)**. Click **OK**.

8. Click **Vaults...** and select **Vault_Training**. Click **OK**. The New User dialog box should display as shown below.

9. Click **OK**.

10. Create other users with a *User Name* of **user2** using the same roles and vault as defined for user1.

11. Click **OK**. Close the dialog boxes.

12. Close the Autodesk Data Management Server Console.

13. Log in to Autodesk Vault client, **Vault_Training** vault as Administrator, no password.

14. For Vault Revision Table. click **Tools>Administration>Vault Settings**. In the Vault Settings dialog box, select the *Behaviors* tab and click **Revision Table.**

15. In the Revision Table Settings dialog box, select the **Enable Revision Table Control** checkbox to enable the Vault Revision Table Functionality.

16. Select **Tools>Administration>Global Settings**.

17. Select the *Change Orders* tab and then click **Define**. In the Routing window, click **Edit** to edit the Default Routing. Select **user1** and add all of the available roles to **user1**, as shown below.

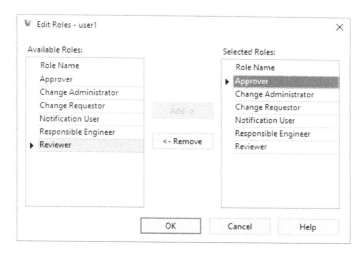

18. Close the dialog boxes.

Chapter
1

Introduction to Autodesk Vault

Autodesk® Vault is Product Lifecycle Management software (PLM) that enables you to secure, consolidate, and organize all product information for easy reference, sharing, and reuse. Autodesk Vault users can store and search both non-CAD data (such as Microsoft® Word and Microsoft® Excel® files) and CAD data (such as Autodesk® Inventor®, AutoCAD®, and DWF files). In this chapter, you learn about the features in the Autodesk Vault software to manage your Autodesk Inventor designs.

Learning Objectives in this Chapter

- Describe the key features and benefits of the Autodesk Vault software.
- Differentiate between terms used in the Autodesk Vault software.
- Identify the ways that Autodesk Vault functions can be accessed.

1.1 Autodesk Vault Features

Autodesk Vault is Product Lifecycle Management (PLM) software that manages the life of a design from conception to retirement. The files associated with the design are tracked and managed. The software also manages who is permitted to work with files at specific times.

The Autodesk Vault software's capabilities include:

- Central repository for data.

- Security access control to data.

- Protection against accidentally overwriting design data.

- Object relationship management.

- Tracks revision history.

- Search and view tools to easily find and view design data.

- Manages CAD and non-CAD data.

- Direct CAD Integration with Autodesk CAD products: Autodesk Inventor, AutoCAD, AutoCAD Mechanical, AutoCAD® Civil 3D®, and many more.

- Copy Design tool for copying an entire design, including all related files, and maintaining their relationships to each other in the new design.

- Change Management functionality.

- Items/Bill of Materials Management.

This student guide focuses on the core functionality of the Autodesk Vault Professional software from a user's perspective.

1.2 Terms and Definitions

Before working with the software, it is recommended to become familiar with the fundamental terminology of the Autodesk Vault software. This section describes some of the commonly used Autodesk Vault terminology.

Object

Object is a generic term used to describe anything stored in the Autodesk Vault database, such as files and items.

File

File is the term used to describe files stored in the Autodesk Vault database. The vault can store any type of file, including Autodesk Inventor, Project files, AutoCAD, AutoCAD Mechanical, AutoCAD Civil 3D, Microsoft Excel, Microsoft Word, etc.

By default, files stored in the Autodesk Vault database do not require unique filenames. Select **Tools>Administration>Vault Settings** and select **Enforce Unique File Names** to ensure that the filenames are unique in the Autodesk Vault software, as shown in Figure 1–1.

Figure 1–1

> ### Best Practice: Using Unique Filenames
>
> Enforcing unique filenames is a recommended best practice. If not previously enforced, you can search for duplicates by clicking **Find Duplicates**.

Item

An Item is an object type that represents all information related to the end item part. It is a container for data that can include Autodesk Inventor files (and other associated reference files), ECOs, and BOMs. Items refer to what a company manages, assembles, sells, and manufactures. An item is identified by its item number or part number. Not only can items represent parts and assemblies, they can also represent paint, lubricants, etc.

Change Order

A Change Order, also referred to as an ECO, is an object that describes why, how, and when changes are made to an Item and/or Inventor file. The result and purpose of a Change Order is to release these objects.

Properties / Metadata

Object properties refer to the information or metadata associated with a specific object in the Autodesk Vault database. Every object in the database has properties that include the object name, state, revision, version, and other attributes. Since the Autodesk Vault software stores these properties in the database, they can be searched for to locate an object.

File Management Terminology

Autodesk Vault's operations include recording the process of change in a file. The terminology related to these processes is described as follows:

Term	Description
Get	Downloads a copy of a file from the vault into a client's working folder. This option enables you to either get a read-only copy of the files, or mark the file as being worked on (checked out) so that you can make modifications. The Autodesk Vault software always contains the master copy of the file.
Check Out	Marks the file as being worked on (checked out) but does not download a copy to your working folder.
Undo Check Out	Checks the selected files back in, unmodified, without creating a new version and without uploading the files back to the vault.

Check In	Uploads a file from the client's working folder to the Autodesk Vault database. You are prompted to save a file before check in if you have not already done so.
Open	Opens the latest version of a file in the associated application. It downloads a copy of the file from the vault into a client's working folder.
Version	Defines the state of the file in the change process. It is an incremental numeric attribute that changes every time a file is changed and submitted (checked in) to the database.
Working Copy	A local copy of the file that has been downloaded from the vault and is located in a local directory or workspace on your machine. The downloading takes place during **Get** and **Open** operations.
File Status in Vault (Vault Status)	Defined by both the state of the file (checked in, checked out, etc.) and the state of the file in the vault compared to the local copy on the client's file system (newer, older, etc.).
Refresh	Updates the current state of the files in the vault.
Revision	Defines a collection of versions with a single character typically, such as A or B. A revision is created with the Revise command. Revisions can also be automatically generated through a Lifecycle State change.

Best Practice: Delete Working Copies

The vault contains all of the master files, which means you are working on a copy of the master file each time you check it out. When you check a file back into the Vault, it becomes the latest version of the master file. Consider your workspace or local working folders as a temporary location for your design files as they are being modified. A recommended best practice is to delete the working copies when you check them in.

Category

Categories are used to group objects and help to assign behaviors and rules to each group of objects. A category can automatically assign user-defined properties to objects in the Vault. Categories can also be used to automatically assign lifecycle definitions or revision values to files.

Lifecycle

Lifecycles are used to manage the stages of maturity of an object. Objects such as files, items and change orders move from state to state (e.g., Work in Progress > For Review > Released, etc.), as managed by the lifecycle definition. At each lifecycle state, an individual is responsible for performing some type of work. An example of a file or item lifecycle is shown in Figure 1–2. An example of a change order object or ECO lifecycle is shown in Figure 1–3.

File or Item Lifecycle Example

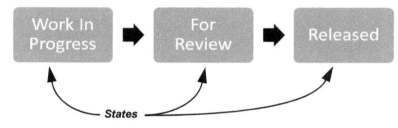

Figure 1–2

ECO (Change Order) Lifecycle Example

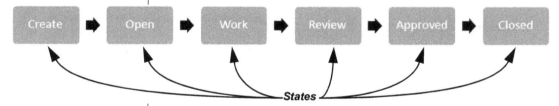

Figure 1–3

1.3 Accessing Autodesk Vault

There are two ways of accessing Autodesk Vault functions:

* Logging in to the Autodesk Vault client.

* Logging in from Autodesk Inventor to use the Autodesk Inventor Vault Add-in.

Autodesk Vault Client

The Autodesk Vault client (also referred to as Autodesk Vault Explorer), provides the user interface for accessing data in the vault. Tasks performed in the Autodesk Vault client software include searching the vault, viewing file status and history, and checking files in and out. The Autodesk Vault software can also be launched and accessed from the Autodesk Inventor software.

The Autodesk Vault client software displays a complete view of the data in the vault. The main window includes the Navigation pane, Main table, Preview pane, and Properties grid, as shown in Figure 1–4.

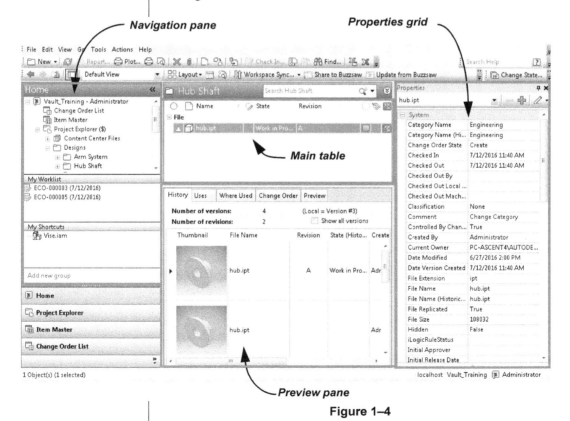

Figure 1–4

Autodesk Inventor Vault Add-in

The Autodesk Inventor software has a direct integration with Autodesk Vault using the Autodesk Inventor Vault Add-in. This means that the Autodesk Inventor software has a Vault menu or tab in its interface, providing quick access to the Autodesk Vault options. File operations, such as Check In and Check Out, can be performed from within the Autodesk Inventor interface to maintain file relationship integrity. The integration interface showing the Vault menu is shown in Figure 1–5.

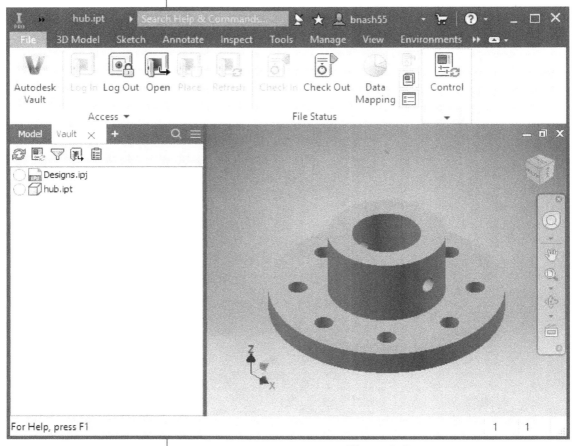

Figure 1–5

Chapter Review Questions

1. What are some of the key features and benefits of the Autodesk Vault software?
   a. Central repository for data.
   b. Protection against accidentally overwriting design data.
   c. Search and display tools to easily find and view design data.
   d. All of the above.

2. What term is used to describe the stages of maturity of an object?
   a. Item
   b. Change Order
   c. Lifecycle
   d. Revision

3. The **Check Out** command downloads a copy of a file from the vault into a client's working folder.
   a. True
   b. False

4. Which of the following provides a complete view of all of the data files in the vault?
   a. Autodesk Vault Client (also known as Autodesk Vault Explorer)
   b. Autodesk Data Management Console
   c. Autodesk Inventor
   d. Vault Add-in

5. What term relates to the incremental numeric attribute that changes every time a file is changed, submitted, and checked in to the database?
   a. State
   b. Revision
   c. Version
   d. File Status

6. In Figure 1–6, what is the name of the highlighted area?

   a. Navigation Pane

   b. Preview Pane

   c. Main Table

   d. Properties Grid

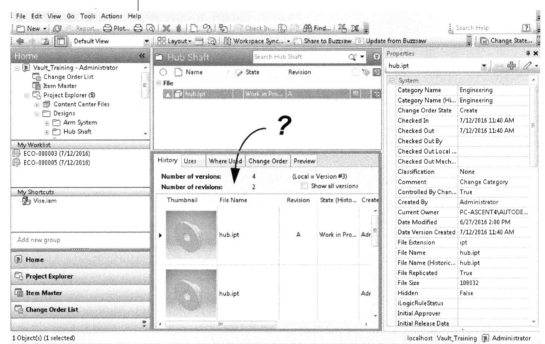

Figure 1–6

Chapter

2

Orientation to Autodesk Vault

This chapter takes you through the process of logging into the Autodesk® Vault client software, setting up the vault folder structure, familiarizing yourself with the interface and accessing data, and then adding non-CAD files to the vault.

Learning Objectives in this Chapter

- Log in to the Autodesk Vault client.
- Set the vault working folder.
- Set up the vault folder structure in the Autodesk Vault software.
- Differentiate between the main areas of the Autodesk Vault interface.
- Describe the functions of each main area of the Autodesk Vault interface.
- Add non-CAD files to the Autodesk Vault software using the Add Files command and the drag and drop method.

2.1 Logging in to the Autodesk Vault Client

Use the following steps to log in to the Autodesk Vault client software. Once logged in, you have access to the metadata and physical files.

How To: Log in to the Autodesk Vault Client

1. The Autodesk Vault client can be started using one of the following methods:

   - Double-click on ![PRO] (Autodesk Vault Professional 2018) on the desktop.
   - Select **Start>All Programs>Autodesk>Autodesk Data Management>Autodesk Vault 2018**.

2. In the Log In dialog box, enter the *User Name* and *Password* as shown in Figure 2–1.

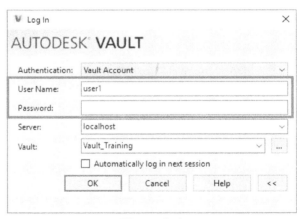

Figure 2–1

3. In the Server drop-down list, select the server, as required.
4. In the Vault drop-down list, select the vault, as required. You can also click ![...] (Browse) to display the list of active vaults.
5. Select **Automatically Log in next session**. In subsequent sessions, this enables you to be automatically logged into the vault as the previous specified user.
6. Click **OK**.

2.2 Folder Structure

After logging in to the Autodesk Vault client for the first time, you should familiarize yourself with the vault folder structure and associated client folders in the Navigation pane.

Vault Folders

The Root in the Autodesk Vault client (also known as the Project Explorer Root) is the top-level directory and is defined as $. Typically, a *Designs* folder or project folders are created below the Root to hold all of your designs. Library folders contain read-only library parts and require their own folder structure, separate from the *Designs* folder structure. They must also be located directly below the Root.

Working Folder

The working folder is a location on the client machine to which design files are copied when they have been either copied as read-only or checked out of the database using the **Get** command.

The working folder is set for the Root of the vault and not for each folder. This is because the folder structure used in the vault is automatically replicated below the working folder on the client's machine when using the **Get** command. When the Autodesk Vault client software is installed, a working folder is defined by default so that you can begin working with a vault. The default working folder is *My Documents>Vault*.

A new working folder can be defined if a consistent working folder for all users has not been enforced by the system administrator. If the administrator has enforced a consistent working folder, a warning message opens indicating that the working folder cannot be changed if you try to set a new one.

By default, the working folder path is not displayed in the title bar. To display the path, select **Tools>Options** and select the **Show working folder location** option.

Best Practice: Store Files Temporarily in Working Folder

As a recommended best practice, the working folder should be considered a temporary folder in which to store files until they are checked back into the vault. Once checked back into the vault, the files should be deleted.

How To: Set Up the Vault Folder Structure

1. Set the working folder if it has not already been enforced by the system administrator. To set the working folder, select the root of the vault and select **File>Set Working Folder**, as shown in Figure 2–2.

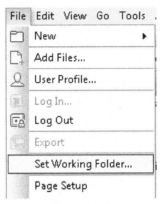

Figure 2–2

A working folder is set up for each user, machine, and vault.

2. Browse to the folder on your machine that is at the top-level directory of all of your design folders. Click **OK** when the design folder is selected. If the folder does not exist, you can create one by clicking **Make New Folder**.
3. Create the top-level design folder if it has not already been created. Select the Project Explorer Root, right-click on it, and select **New Folder**, as shown in Figure 2–3.

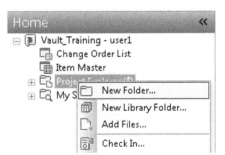

Figure 2–3

You can create as many subfolders for each design as required. If a folder hierarchy does exist on the local machine, the folder hierarchy in the vault should match for simplicity. However, if vault folders do not have a match on the local machine, the folder structure on the local machine is replicated to match the vault folder structure, as required, when using the **Get** command.

Similarly, if the *Designs* local folder structure contains additional subfolders in preparation for adding designs to the vault, these subfolders are automatically created (as required) in the vault as files are added. When you have created the required folders, you might need to make corrections or modifications to the folder structure, such as renaming or deleting folders.

- To rename a folder, right-click on it and select **Rename**.

- To delete a folder, right-click on it and select **Delete**.

4. Create the top-level library folder if it has not already been created. Select the Vault Explorer Root, right-click, and select **New Library Folder**, as shown in Figure 2–4.

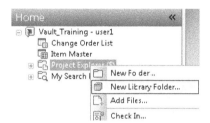

Figure 2–4

Links

Links can be created anywhere in the Project Explorer and point to a target object (such as a file, folder, item, or change order). The target object resides in one location only. Organizing objects and links in a project folder can facilitate management and reporting. Commands such as **Check Out** and **Check In** can be performed using a link and are executed on the target object. Note that the **Delete** and **Move** commands only affect the link and not the target object.

How To: Create a Link

1. Select the target object for the link.
2. In the Edit menu, select **Copy** as shown in Figure 2–5.

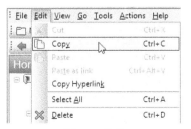

Figure 2–5

3. Select the link's destination folder.
4. In the Edit menu, select **Paste as link** as shown in Figure 2–6.

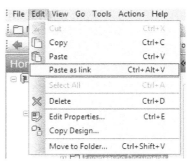

Figure 2–6

5. The link is created in that folder with an arrow included in the entity icon as shown in Figure 2–7.

Figure 2–7

2.3 Autodesk Vault Interface Overview

The Autodesk Vault interface consists of the following main areas, as shown in Figure 2–8:

- Navigation pane

- Main table or pane

- Preview pane

- Properties grid

- Toolbars

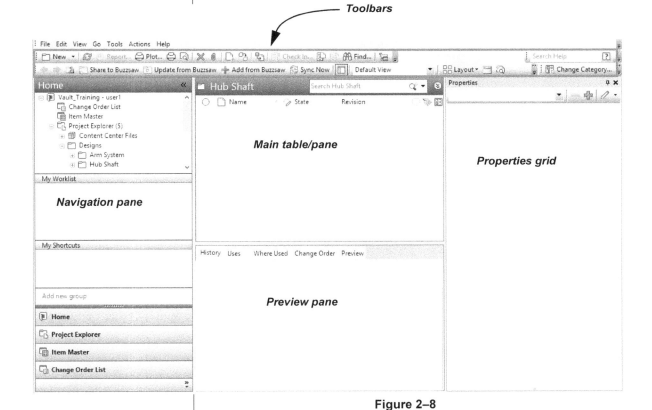

Figure 2–8

The Navigation pane shows the folder structure in a tree format, while the data displays in the Main and Preview panes in a column or grid format. An example is shown in Figure 2–9.

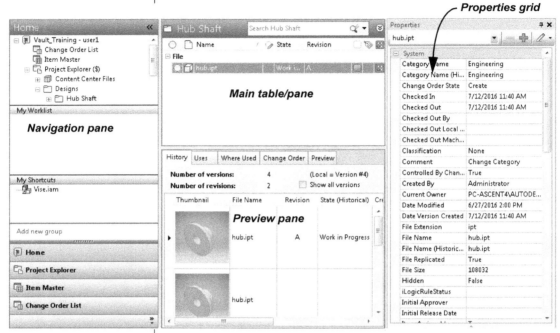

Figure 2–9

2.4 Navigation Pane

The Navigation pane, located on the left side of the interface, contains the *Home*, *Project Explorer*, *Item Master,* and *Change Order List* tabs. The active tab is highlighted in orange. The Project Explorer, Item Master, and Change Order List data can be accessed by clicking on their respective links, or from the *Home* tab, as shown in Figure 2–10.

Figure 2–10

The Project Explorer displays the vault objects in a tree view, as shown in Figure 2–11.

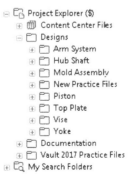

Figure 2–11

The Project Explorer behaves similar to Windows Explorer. Folders with subfolders display ⊞ (Expand) next to each folder name, which you can click to expand the branch. Expanded folders display ⊟ (Collapse), which enables you to collapse the branch when clicked. Right-click on a folder to display the contextual options.

The Project Explorer also contains a folder called *My Search Folders*. You can use this to create saved searches for quick access.

2.5 Main Table

The Main table or pane display changes depending on the tab you are using:

- Using the *Project Explorer* tab, it displays objects that reside in the selected vault folder.

- Using the *Item Master* tab, it displays the Item Master list.

- Using the *Change Order List* tab, it displays the Change Order objects.

Project Explorer

When using the Project Explorer, the vault folder name displays in the Main table title bar. To display the working folder path name instead of just the folder names used, select **Tools>Options** and select **Show working folder location**. The Main table displaying files and the local working folder path is shown in Figure 2–12.

Displays the vault folder name and the path to the folder

Figure 2–12

The default columns that display include: *Vault Status, Entity Icon, Name, State, Revision, Category Glyph, Property Compliance,* and *Linked to Item*.

It is a best practice to keep the DWF files hidden. If they display during checkout, they are also checked out.

By default, automatically generated .DWF files are hidden in the list. To display the .DWF file, select **Tools>Options** and then select **Show hidden files** in the Options dialog box.

You can customize the columns in the Main table to show, remove, reorder, and sort additional file properties as required by right-clicking on a column header and using the **Customize View>Fields** option.

Item Master

If the *Item Master* tab is selected, the Main table displays the items in the table. The default columns that display include: *Vault Status, Number, Revision, State, Title (Item, CO), Category Glyph, Property Compliance,* and *Controlled by Change Order,* as shown in Figure 2–13.

Figure 2–13

Change Order List

If the *Change Order List* tab is selected, the main table displays the Change Order objects in the table. The default columns that display include: *Vault Status, Number of File Attachments, Number, State, Title (Item, CO),* and *Due Date,* as shown in Figure 2–14.

Figure 2–14

2.6 Preview Pane

The Preview pane is one of three main areas in the Autodesk Vault interface (the other two are the Navigation pane and the Main table). When a file is selected, the Preview pane displays information, which is categorized into tabs. These tabs are different for the Project Explorer, Item Master, and Change Order list.

Project Explorer

When using the Project Explorer, the tabs are: *History, Uses, Where Used,* and *Preview.*

History Tab

The *History* tab displays versions of the file that has been selected in the Main table. File properties display for each version. The default properties displayed include the *Thumbnail, File Name, Version, Created By* (which user checked in the file), *Checked In* (date of the version), and *Comment,* as shown in Figure 2–15.

Figure 2–15

You can customize the columns to show, remove, reorder, and sort additional file properties as required by right-clicking on a column header and using the **Customize View>Fields** option.

Uses Tab

The *Uses* tab lists all of the files used in the selected file as shown in Figure 2–16. The Revision drop-down list enables you to see files that were used throughout the history of the selected file.

Figure 2–16

Where Used Tab

The *Where Used* tab displays files in the vault that reference the selected file, as shown in Figure 2–17.

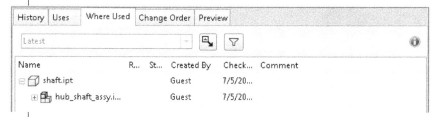

Figure 2–17

Click ⓘ (Parents Loaded) to display the Direct and Total number of parents loaded. Use the Revision drop-down list to display where the selected file has been used throughout its history.

Preview Tab

The *Preview* tab displays a carousel view of the selected file, as shown in Figure 2–18. The carousel view enables you to view thumbnails of the selected file and cycle through previous versions of the file in Vault Basic, or previous revisions and versions of the file in Vault Professional. The file version or revision displays at the top of each thumbnail, and the last check-in date displays at the bottom.

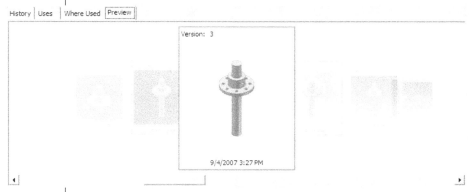

Figure 2–18

For files (such as parts, assemblies, and Autodesk Inventor drawings), Autodesk Vault attaches a visualization file to the selected file. When the thumbnail is selected, the associated visualization file is loaded using the Autodesk DWF Viewer (.IPT, .IAM, or .IDW) or a document previewer (.DOC, .XLS, .PPT, .XPS, .CSV, or .ZIP). The .DWF file can be automatically generated for Autodesk Inventor models. When you select a previous version of a file a warning displays, as shown in Figure 2–19.

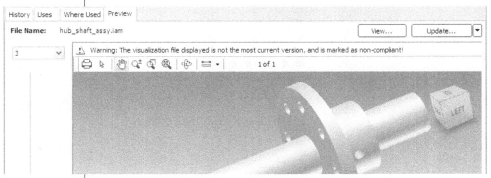

Figure 2–19

The DWF Viewer enables you to rotate, zoom, pan, print, and measure .DWF images. Use the version slider to display the history of the file.

The following DWF Viewer icons display in the Preview pane> *Preview* tab:

Icon	Description
	Pan the Canvas: Enables you to move around the model.
	Zoom In/Out: Enables you to zoom in or out of the model.
	Zoom Area: Enables you to use a selection window to zoom to a specific area in the Preview window.
	Fit to Window: Enables you to fit the model into the Preview window.
	Orbit: Enables you to rotate the model.
	Measure Length: Enables you to measure objects on the model.

Non-DWF documents can also be previewed, including the following file formats:

- Microsoft® Office Word (.DOC, .DOCX, .DOT, .DOTX, and .RTF)

- Microsoft® Office Excel® (.XLS, .XLSB, .XLSX, and .XLTX)

- Microsoft® Office PowerPoint® (.POT, .POTX, .PPS, .PPSX, .PPT, and .PPTX)

- Microsoft® Outlook® Email previewer (*.msg)

- PDF preview handler (.PDF)

- XPS viewer (.XPS)

- Comma separated values (.CSV)

- Compressed files (.ZIP)

To control which application will be used as the default viewer for the various file formats, select **Tools>Options** and click **Document Previewers...**.

For files that cannot be viewed with the DWF Viewer or a document viewer, right-click and select **Open**, select **File>Open**, or click **Open** in the Preview pane to launch the associated application and display the file.

Item Master

For *Item Master*, the tabs are: *General*, *History*, *Bill of Materials*, *Where Used*, *Change Order*, and *View*.

Additional details will be covered in the Items and Bill of Materials Management chapter.

Change Order List

For *Change Order List*, the tabs are: *General*, *Records*, *Comments*, *Files*, *Routing*, and *Status*.

Additional details will be covered in the Change Management chapter.

2.7 Properties Grid

You can display Properties in the Properties Grid, as shown in Figure 2–20.

Figure 2–20

To manage file properties, select **Tools>Administration>Vault Settings**, and then in the *Behaviors* tab, click **Properties**. The Property Definitions dialog box opens, as shown in Figure 2–21.

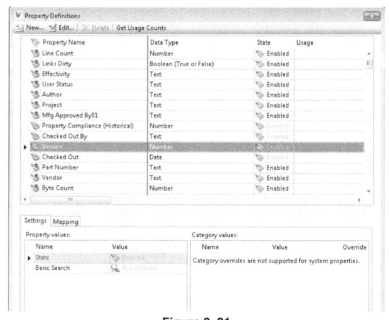

Figure 2–21

2.8 Toolbars

Autodesk Vault's standard and advanced toolbars, shown in Figure 2–22, provide fast access to many vault operations.

Standard toolbar

Advanced toolbar

Figure 2–22

The icons available depend on the files selected in the Main table.

Standard Toolbar Icons

Icon	Description
New ▾	**New Folder** or **New Library Folder:** Creates a new folder or new library area.
	Refresh: Updates the current state of the files in the vault.
Report...	**Report:** Create report using selected template.
Plot...	**Plot:** Plots selected files.
	Print Direct: Prints directly to the printer.
	Print Preview: Previews the output before it is printed.
	Delete: Deletes the selected files.
	Attachments: Select a file and view its attachment or attach additional files, as required.
	Add Files: Adds files to the vault.
	Copy Design: Copies an entire design, including all of the related files, parts, drawings, subassemblies, and attachments to a new design.
Check In...	**Check In:** Checks in the selected files.
	Get: Downloads the selected files from the vault to the working folder and are read only by default.
	Undo Check Out: Undoes the **Check Out** operation on selected files.

🔍 Find...	**Find:** Searches the vault by entering a specified text string.
	Autodesk App Store Manager: Launches the Autodesk App Store Manager to view and manage your Autodesk Apps.

Advanced Toolbar Icons

Icon	Description
⬅	**Move Backward:** Moves you back to the previously selected folder in the Navigation pane.
➡	**Move Forward:** After moving backwards, click to return to the folder in which you started.
⬆	**Up One Level:** Moves you back to the parent of the selected folder in the Navigation pane.
⬚	**Preview Pane:** Toggles the Preview pane on and off.
Default View ▾	Controls whether the default view or a custom view is assigned to control the display of the Main Table.
⊞ Layout ▾	**Layout:** Controls the display of files in the Main Table. Options include **Detail View**, **Small Icons**, or **Large Icons**.
⬒	**Group By Box:** Groups column headings.
🔍	**Auto Preview:** Displays comments for each file on a separate line below the file details.
⬆ Workspace Sync... ▾	**Workspace Sync:** Synchronizes the contents of your local workspace with the contents of the corresponding Vault folders.
🗂 Change Category...	**Change Category:** Changes the category of the selected object.
🗂 Change State...	**Change State:** Changes the state of the selected object.
🗂 Change Revision...	**Change Revision:** Changes the Revision of the selected object.

2.9 Adding Non-CAD Files to the Vault

You can add any file format to a vault. When a file is added, it is transferred to the vault and becomes the master file.

Your user role must be defined as Editor or Administrator to add files to the vault.

If CAD files are added using the Autodesk Vault interface, the relationship between Autodesk Inventor files, or the relationship between a DWG host file and its xrefs are not tracked. Instead, the respective Vault Add-in software should be used for this purpose.

*   You can use Vault Explorer for non-CAD files.

How To: Add a Non-CAD File to the Vault

You can also drag and drop files from Windows Explorer to the Autodesk Vault software to add non-CAD files to the vault.

1. Select the vault folder in which you want the file to be stored.
2. Right-click and select **Add Files**.
3. Navigate to the folder in which the file is located and select the file. Click **Open**.
4. In the Add Files dialog box, select **Keep files checked out** if you want to check the file out immediately after you check it in. For example, you could use this option at the end of the work day. This ensures that the modified file is in the vault for backup and is available for viewing, but remains checked out so that you can continue with the modifications. This prevents others from checking out and changing the file.
5. Select **Delete working copies** to delete the file from your computer. This is a recommended best practice if you have finished modifying the file. When you need to modify it again or to view the file, you can retrieve it from the vault to ensure you are working with the latest.
6. In the *Enter comments to include...* area, type a description of the file, such as **Initial submission to vault**.
7. Click **OK** add the file to the vault.

Once added to the vault, the file displays in the Main table. The *Vault Status* column indicates that the file is available for check out. If the local copy was deleted, the column indicates that you do not have a local copy.

Practice 2a	Orientation to Autodesk Vault

Practice Objectives

- Log in to the Autodesk Vault software and set a working folder.
- Compare the working folder structure to the vault folder structure.
- View and analyze vaulted files.

In this practice, you will log in to the Autodesk Vault software and become familiar with the user interface. You will also set a working folder and compare the folder structure on the local machine to the vault folder structure.

Task 1 - Log in to the Autodesk Vault software.

1. Log in to the Autodesk Vault software using one of the following methods:

   - Double-click on  (Autodesk Vault 2018) on the desktop.
   - Select **Start>All Programs>Autodesk>Autodesk Data Management>Autodesk Vault 2018**.

Refer to the Practice Files section of this student guide to setup the Vault, if not already completed.

2. The Log In dialog box opens as shown in Figure 2–23. In the *User Name* field, type **user1**. Verify that *Vault* is set to **Vault_Training** (click ⌶⋯⌷ (Browse) to select it, as required). Leave the *Password* field blank.

Figure 2–23

Selecting this option saves login time.

3. Select **Automatically log in next session** to automatically logged into the vault in subsequent sessions.

4. Click **OK**.

Task 2 - Set a new working folder.

In this task, you will set a new working folder. The vault database has been created with the *Content Center Files*, *Designs*, and *Documentation* folders created in the Project Explorer ($) root.

1. Select **Project Explorer ($)** and select **File>Set Working Folder**.

2. In the Browse For Folder dialog box, select **C:\Vault Data Management Practice Files\vault_work** and click **OK**.

3. The working folder path can be displayed in the Main table's title bar. To display the path, if not already displayed, select **Tools>Options** and select **Show working folder location**. Click **OK**. Verify that the path is set to *...\vault_work*.

Task 3 - Compare folder structures.

In this task, you will compare the folder structure in the working folder (*...\vault_work*) to the Vault folder structure.

1. To view the working folder, select **Actions>Go To Working Folder**. Windows Explorer opens displaying the working folder contents. Note that there is no *Hub Shaft* subfolder under the *Designs* folder in the local working folder structure.

2. In the Autodesk Vault software, expand **Project Explorer ($)>Designs**. Note that the subfolders in vault are different. Only Hub Shaft exists in the vault.

3. Close Windows Explorer.

Task 4 - View files in the vault.

In this task, you will use the Preview pane to view and analyze an assembly design.

1. In the *Designs>Hub Shaft* folder, select **hub_shaft_assy.iam**.

*If the preview does not display, click **Update...** to create the .DWF preview file.*

2. In the Preview pane, select the *Preview* tab to view the carousel of versions for this assembly. Select **Version 5** to view the visualization file of this version.

3. Use the ViewCube or the icons at the top of the viewer to manipulate and analyze the assembly.

4. In the *Preview* tab, expand the Versions drop-down list and select **Version 1** to display Version 1 of the assembly. The shaft length is shorter in Version 1.

5. Select the *History* tab and select the **Show all versions** checkbox to view the history of the assembly versions. The *Comment* column for Version 2 states that the shaft length was changed, as shown in Figure 2–24.

Figure 2–24

6. Select the *Uses* and *Where Used* tabs to display any children and whether any parents are associated with the selected file.

Practice 2b

Adding Non-CAD Files to the Vault

Practice Objectives

- Add a non-CAD file to the vault using the Add Files command, or the drag and drop method.
- View a non-CAD file in the vault.

In this practice, you will add non-CAD files to the vault and then display them.

Task 1 - Add non-CAD files to the vault using Add Files.

In this task, you will add a PDF file to the vault using the Add Files command.

1. In the Navigation pane, select the $\$\Documentation$ folder, right-click, and select **Add Files**.

2. In the *C:\Vault Data Management Practice Files\vault_work\ Documentation* folder, select the document **Using Autodesk Vault with Single Inventor Project.pdf**, and click **Open**.

3. In the Add Files... dialog box, select **Delete working copies**. In the *Enter comments to include...* area, enter **Initial submission** as shown in Figure 2–25.

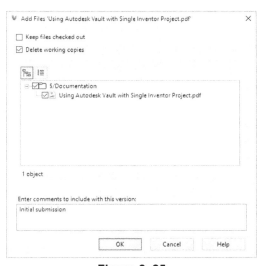

Figure 2–25

4. Click **OK**.

Task 2 - Add non-CAD files to the vault using drag and drop.

In this task, you will add a Word file to the vault using drag and drop.

1. In the Navigation pane, select the $\Documentation folder to view its current files.

2. In a Windows Explorer window, navigate to the C:\Vault Data Management Practice Files\vault_work\Documentation\ folder.

3. Drag **Software Setup.docx and drop it into the vault Documentation folder**.

4. In the Add Files... dialog box, select **Delete working copies**. In the Enter comments to include... area, enter **Initial submission** as shown in Figure 2–26.

Figure 2–26

5. Click **OK**.

Task 3 - View the non-CAD files in the vault.

In this task, you will view the non-CAD files in the vault.

1. In the Main table, select the document **Using Autodesk Vault with Single Inventor Project.pdf**.

2. Switch to the *Preview* tab to display the thumbnail of Version 1. Click the thumbnail to display the PDF in the Preview pane.

3. In the *Preview* tab, click **Open** to open the PDF file in a PDF viewing program outside the Vault.

4. Close the window displaying the PDF file.

5. In the Main table, select **Software Setup.docx**. Click the thumbnail in the *Preview* tab to display the document in the Preview pane.

Chapter Review Questions

1. What is a working folder?

   a. Central repository for data.

   b. A location on the client machine to which design files are downloaded from the vault.

   c. A location in the vault that contains your design files.

   d. All of the above.

2. What are the main areas of the Autodesk Vault interface? (Select all that apply.)

   a. Navigation Pane.

   b. Main Table

   c. Preview Pane

   d. Properties Grid

   e. Toolbars

3. In the Preview pane, the *Where Used* tab lists all of the files used in the selected file.

   a. True

   b. False

4. In the Preview pane, what does the *Uses* tab display when a file is selected from the Project Explorer?

   a. The files that use the selected file.

   b. The files used in the selected file.

   c. The files that reference the selected file.

   d. Only files that are available to use in the selected file.

5. In the Preview pane, the latest version of the selected file displays in the *Preview* tab by default.

   a. True

   b. False

6. Which file format is used for the *Preview* tab to display an image of an Autodesk Inventor file?

   a. DWF

   b. PRT

   c. DWG

   d. PDF

7. How can a non-CAD file be added to the vault for the first time? (Select all that apply.)

   a. Use the **Check In** command.

   b. Drag and drop from Windows Explorer.

   c. Use the **Add Files** command.

   d. Use the **New Folder** command.

Command Summary

Button	Command	Location
	Add Files	• Standard toolbar
	Attachments	• Standard toolbar
	Auto Preview	• Advanced toolbar
	Autodesk App Store Manager	• Standard toolbar
Check In...	Check In	• Standard toolbar
	Copy Design	• Standard toolbar
	Delete	• Standard toolbar
	Expand the query builder	• Main Table pane
Find...	Find	• Standard toolbar
	Fit to Window	• Preview pane
	Get	• Standard toolbar
	Group By Box	• Advanced toolbar
Layout ▾	Layout	• Advanced toolbar
	Measure Length	• Preview pane
	Move Backward	• Advanced toolbar
	Move Forward	• Advanced toolbar
New ▾	New Folder or New Library Folder	• Standard toolbar
	Orbit	• Preview pane
	Pan the Canvas	• Preview pane
	Preview pane	• Advanced toolbar
	Print Direct	• Standard toolbar
	Print Preview	• Standard toolbar

	Refresh	• Standard toolbar
	Undo Check Out	• Standard toolbar
	Up One Level	• Advanced toolbar
	Zoom Area	• Preview pane
	Zoom In/Out	• Preview pane

Orientation to the Autodesk Inventor Vault Integration Add-in

The Autodesk Inventor Vault Integration software, a Vault Add-in for the Autodesk® Inventor® software, provides direct access to the Autodesk® Vault software in the Autodesk Inventor interface. This integration enables you to perform many of the tasks available using the Autodesk Vault software. In this chapter, you learn about the Autodesk Inventor Vault Integration interface, how to create a vault project, and how to check in Autodesk Inventor files to the vault.

Learning Objectives in this Chapter

- Configure the integration between Autodesk Inventor and Autodesk Vault by creating a vault master project file and mapping your local folder structure to the vault.
- Log in to the Autodesk Vault software from the Autodesk Inventor software.
- Differentiate between using Open in the Quick Access Toolbar and Open in the *Vault* tab, in the Access panel.
- Check the status of Autodesk Inventor files located in the vault using the Vault Browser in the Autodesk Inventor software.
- Use the Check In and Check In Project commands to upload Autodesk Inventor files to the vault.

3.1 Autodesk Vault Projects

When working with the Autodesk Inventor software, projects are used for organizing and accessing all files that are associated with a particular design job. When you are using Inventor with the Autodesk Vault software, the project must be an Autodesk Vault project rather than an Autodesk Inventor project. The key difference between an Autodesk Inventor project file and an Autodesk Vault project file is that workgroup search paths are not permitted in the Autodesk Vault project files. You must consolidate all of the project folders under the single workspace search path for the project.

One method of integrating an Autodesk Vault project into your Autodesk Inventor environment is to use the single project or *vault master project* method. This uses one project file for the entire vault instead of setting up separate project files for each project/design. With the single project method, you create a folder for each design with all designs referencing one master project file. Recommended by Autodesk, the single project method is the simplest and most robust way of setting up your Autodesk Inventor Vault integration.

The vault master project file can be located under the Project Explorer Root ($) or in a subfolder under Project Explorer Root ($). When you want to work with the vault, use this vault project file.

How To: Create a Vault Master Project File

1. In the Autodesk Inventor software, in the *Get Started* tab> Launch panel, click 🗂 (Projects). The Project Editor opens as shown in Figure 3–1.

*You can also click **Projects...** from the Open dialog box to display the Project Editor.*

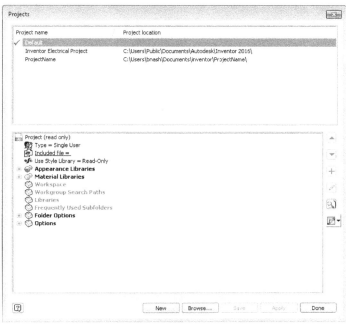

Figure 3–1

2. Click **New** to create a project file.
3. Select **New Vault Project** and click **Next**.
4. Enter the Project Name and specify the location of the project file, as shown in Figure 3–2.

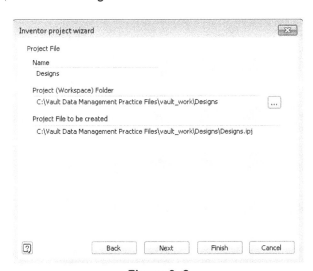

Figure 3–2

5. Click **Next** and click **Finish**.
6. Expand Folder Options, right-click on the *Content Center Files* folder, and select **Edit**, as shown in Figure 3–3. Enter the new Content Center Files directory path.

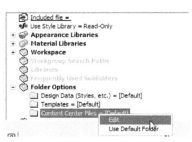

Figure 3–3

7. Specify any other settings, such as locations for the styles library, templates, etc.
8. Click **Save** to save the changes to the project file.
9. In the Project Editor, double-click on the project name and then click **Done** to make the new project active.

A default project file can be set by your administrator, otherwise Autodesk Inventor's last vault controlled project file is used.

The project file is created in the specified location, but is not added to the vault. You add the project file to the vault after you map the folders. With a single project file, there is no need for each user to create a master project file. They only need to perform a **Get** operation on the single vault master project file and then activate it in the Autodesk Inventor software.

3.2 Mapping Folders

When you add or access Autodesk Inventor files in the vault, the local folder paths displayed in the project file need to match the folders in the vault. The Autodesk Inventor software uses this information when storing the files. The information is then saved in the master project file. The Project Root mapping displays in the project file in the **Vault Options>Virtual Folder** branch, as shown in Figure 3–4.

Figure 3–4

How To: Map the Local Folder Structure to the Vault

1. In the Autodesk Inventor software, in the *Vault* tab, expand the Access panel and click ⬚ (Map Folders) as shown in Figure 3–5.

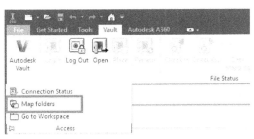

Figure 3–5

2. The Project Folder Mapping dialog box opens, as shown in Figure 3–6. Map the Project Root and Content Center Files directories to specific folders in the vault.

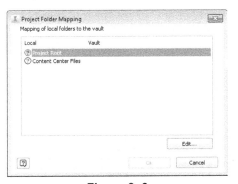

Figure 3–6

3. Select **Project Root** and click **Edit...**. The Browse Vault for Folder dialog box opens, listing the folders currently in the vault.
4. Select the *Designs* folder and click **OK**.
5. Select **Content Center Files** and click **Edit...**.
6. In the Browse Vault for Folder dialog box, select the *Content Center Files* folder and click **OK**.
7. Click **OK** to complete the mapping changes and close the Project Folder Mapping dialog box. The vault folders are now mapped for your workspace.

3.3 Log in to Vault from Autodesk Inventor

When you have set up the master project file and mapped your folder paths, you can log in to the Autodesk Vault software from the Autodesk Inventor interface.

How To: Launch Autodesk Inventor and Log In to the Vault

1. Launch the Autodesk Inventor software.

2. In the *Get Started* tab>Launch panel, click 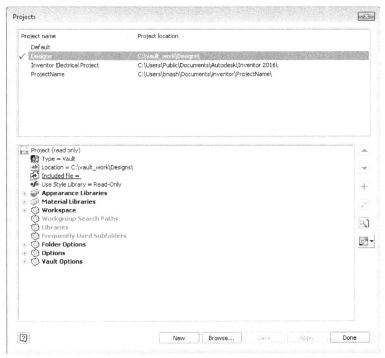 (Projects).
3. In the Projects dialog box, double-click on an Autodesk Vault Project to activate it and click **Done**, as shown in Figure 3–7. You have to create an Autodesk Vault Project if one does not exist.

Figure 3–7

4. In the *Vault* tab>Access panel, click 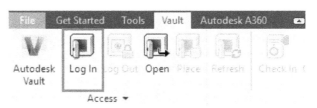 (Log In) as shown in Figure 3–8.

Figure 3–8

*After you have logged in for the first time, the server and vault names are stored so that the same information displays each time you log in to the vault. Select **Automatically log in next session** to log in automatically and bypass the Log In window.*

5. Enter your user name and password as shown in Figure 3–9.

Figure 3–9

6. Click **OK**.

3.4 Open Autodesk Inventor Files from the Vault

Open From Vault

When you have launched the Autodesk Inventor software and selected the active project file, you can open an Autodesk Inventor file. If you click (Open) in the Quick Access Toolbar, rather than (Open) in the *Vault* tab>Access panel, you are prompted to select a file from the local workspace. The workspace is a local folder that is mapped to the corresponding folder in the vault. The workspace can be a single folder, or can include an hierarchy of subfolders to help organize the design.

The recommended best practice is to use (Open) in the *Vault* tab>Access panel to open the file from the vault instead of from the local working folder. This ensures that you are always working with the latest version of the project.

If you click (Open) without logging in, you are prompted to login.

(Open) in the *Vault* tab>Access panel in the integrated user interface is available after you log in to the vault, as shown in Figure 3–10.

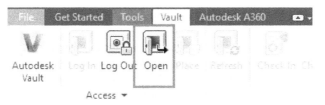

Figure 3–10

How To: Open a File from the Vault

1. In the Autodesk Inventor software, in the *Vault* tab>Access panel, click 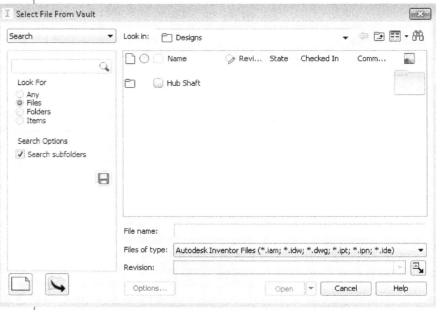 (Open). The Select File From Vault dialog box opens, as shown in Figure 3–11.

Figure 3–11

2. You can navigate the folder structure to select the required file, or you can search using the field shown in Figure 3–12.

You can also locate a file using My Saved Searches or My Shortcuts, as shown in Figure 3–13.

You can use 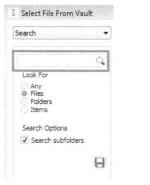 to access the Find dialog box.

Figure 3–12

Figure 3–13

3. To open files in Express mode, select **Options** to open the File Open Options dialog box, and then select **Express**, as shown in Figure 3–14.

Full loads all component data and all commands are available. Express is 3-5x faster when opening large assemblies but some commands are not available.

Figure 3–14

4. Once the file is selected, select  next to **Open** and select one of the open methods, as shown in Figure 3–15.

Figure 3–15

- **Open (Check Out):** Check out and open the file.
- **Open (Check Out All):** Check out and open the selected file and all of its children.
- **Open (Read Only):** Open the file without checking it out.

5. If you do not select one of the methods shown in Figure 3–15, you can click **Open** to retrieve the file from the vault into the Autodesk Inventor software. You are prompted to check out the file.

6. Click **No** to open the file as read-only or click **Yes** and then **OK** to check the file out of the vault.

Place From Vault

To add a component from the vault to an Autodesk Inventor assembly, click (Place) in the *Vault* tab>Access panel. The Select File from Vault dialog box opens.

The options in this dialog box are similar to the ones displayed when **Open From Vault** is selected, with the addition of the iMate functionality when placing components, as shown in Figure 3–16.

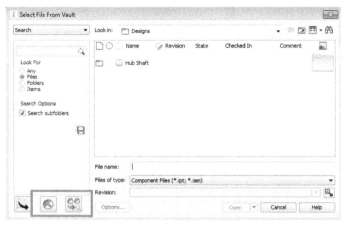

Figure 3–16

Insert into CAD

To place a component from the vault into an Autodesk Inventor design directly from the Autodesk Vault client, use the **Insert into CAD** command. This command downloads the file from the vault and places it into the active Inventor session.

How To: Use the Insert into CAD command

1. In the Autodesk Vault client, select the file to place in the Autodesk Inventor design, right-click, and select **Insert into CAD** as shown in Figure 3–17.

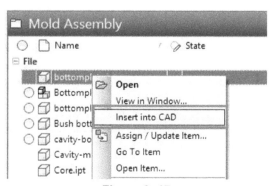

Figure 3–17

2. Finish placing the file into the design.

3.5 Check File Status with Vault Browser

In addition to other operations, the Vault Browser enables you to view the status of Autodesk Inventor files in the vault. In the Autodesk Inventor software, select **Vault** in the Browser panel bar, as shown in Figure 3–18. The Vault Browser opens as shown in Figure 3–19. The Vault Browser toolbar with icons is shown and each component listed in the browser displays a Vault status icon and the filename by default.

Figure 3–18

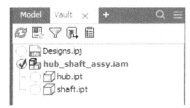
Figure 3–19

The Vault Browser can left undocked, be docked next to the Inventor Browser so that they can be viewed simultaneously, or be moved to float separately.

Vault Browser Toolbar Icons

	Refresh Vault status: Refreshes the file's status to reflect the current state of the files in the vault.
	Update Properties: Updates the properties for the active file and all of its children.
	Filter: Options to filter the Vault Browser display. Options are shown below.

✓ **Vault Status**
   ✓ Checked Out To Me
   ✓ Checked Out To Others
   ✓ Not Checked Out
   ✓ Not In Vault

✓ **Local Files**
   ✓ Without Edits
   ✓ With Saved Edits
   ✓ With Unsaved Edits

	Logged in as: Displays current log in information and launches the Autodesk Vault software.
	Choose Properties: Enables you to specify which Vault Properties display in the Vault Browser after the filename.

Vault Status Icons

- An exclamation mark in a yellow triangle (⚠) indicates that you are not logged into the vault in the Autodesk Inventor software.

- A white circle with a plus sign (⊕) indicates that the files are not in the vault.

- If a filename displays in **blue bold font**, the file is checked out to you. An asterisk beside the filename means that you have changes in memory that have not been saved, and it requires a save before it can be added to the vault.

*When multiple users are working on the same design, use the **Refresh** toolbar icon to see the current status of the loaded files.*

- A white circle containing a checkmark (✓) or nothing (○) indicates that the version of file you are working with is the same as the one in the vault. This is also known as the *Latest Version* and is typically preferred for use.

How To: Use the Vault Browser

1. Hover the cursor over the filename in the Vault Browser to display the vault status tooltip, as shown in Figure 3–20. It provides information on the action that needs to be performed on the file.

Figure 3–20

2. Select a file and right-click to display the shortcut menu. The options available depend on the file format and how the file was opened. For example, if you checked out the file when opening it, the **Check In** option is available but not the **Check Out** one. If you opened the file as **Read Only**, **Check Out** is available.

3. The Vault Browser operation options are described as follows:

Option	Description
Open	Opens the selected file in a new Inventor window.
Refresh File	Downloads a copy of a file's latest checked in version to your local working folder.
Get Revision	Copies a file's selected revision from the vault to the local working folder, enabling it to be modified
Check In	Copies a file from the local working folder to the vault.
Check Out	Copies a file from the vault to the local working folder, enabling it to be modified.
Undo Check Out	Checks the selected files back in, unmodified.
Revert to Latest	Reverts to the latest revision of the file.
Change Category	Changes the category of the selected file.
Change State	Changes the state of the selected file.
Revise	Creates a new revision of the selected file.
Show Details	Opens the Details window displaying a version summary table of the selected component, including the thumbnail image, version number, checked in date, and the name of the user that checked in the version.
Expand All Children	Expands the Vault Browser tree to display the assemblies children (available for assemblies).
Collapse All Children	Collapses the Vault Browser tree to display only the assembly (available for assemblies).
Find in Window	Highlights the selected component in the Autodesk Inventor window.
Go to Vault Folder	Opens a new Vault Explorer session showing the version and revision of the selected component inside its vault folder.

How To: Search in Vault Browser

If Vault properties were added using the Choose Properties dialog box, you can search the value of those properties.

1. To search the contents of the Vault Browser, select the search icon in the browser, as shown in Figure 3–21.

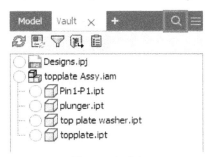

Figure 3–21

Multiple keywords can be entered, separated by a space.

2. Enter a keyword in the *Type Keyword* field, as shown in Figure 3–22.

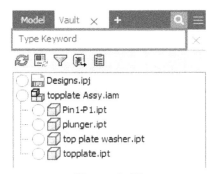

Figure 3–22

Both expanded and collapsed file nodes will be searched.

The results of the keyword search display as shown in Figure 3–23.

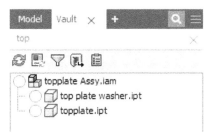

Figure 3–23

3.6 Check In Autodesk Inventor Files to Vault

To maintain parent/child relationships between Autodesk Inventor files, you need to access the Vault directly from the Autodesk Inventor software using either the Vault Browser or the *Vault* tab options (i.e., not using the Autodesk Vault software).

The **Check In** and **Check In Project** operations are used if you are adding files to the vault for the first time. The separate **Autoloader** utility can also be used. Autodesk .DWF files are automatically created and attached for files that have changed or for files that do not already have .DWF files published.

A CAD file becomes the master when it is added or checked into the vault. Use the **Get Revision** operation to update the local working folder with the latest version (leading version of the leading revision) of the selected files. Use **Check Out** when you want to modify the files. These operations copy the requested files to your local working folder again and ensure that you are working with the latest versions.

Best Practice: Temporarily Store Files in the Local Working Folder

As a recommended best practice, the working folder should be considered a temporary folder in which to store files until they are checked back into the vault. Once checked back into the vault, the temporary files should be deleted.

Check In

The **Check In** operation adds files to the vault folders specified during the **Map Folders** operation in the Autodesk Inventor software. These mapped folders are stored in the project file and become the default file storage locations each time you add files. If the files are already in the vault, a Warning box opens.

How To: Check In Files to the Vault

1. After logging into the vault in the Autodesk Inventor software, select the Vault Browser.
2. If the files have been modified, they must be saved before they can be added to the vault. In the Application Menu, expand **Save** and select **Save** or **Save All** to save the files.

It does not matter which file you select, they are all added to the vault.

The vault creates any folders required to support the structure displayed in the dialog box.

3. If a file has not yet been added to the vault, a white circle with a plus sign displays next to it. Select the file, right-click, and select **Check In**. The Check In dialog box displays all of the files that are going to be added to the vault and their folder structure.
4. Select **Keep files checked out** to check the files into the vault and then check them out again so that you can keep working with them.
5. Select **Close files and delete working copies** to close the files after they have been checked in and delete them from the local working folder.
6. Click **Settings** to set the .DWF attachment settings. The **Create visualization attachment** option is selected by default. The **Apply to all files** option is disabled because all of the parts and assemblies are added by default.
7. In the *Enter comments to include...* area, enter comments as required.
8. Click **OK**.

Check In Project

The **Check In Project** operation bulk loads design projects into the vault in one operation, while maintaining file relationships. This operation locates all of the files related to the project using the defined search paths. The files added include the presentations (.IPN), parts (.IPT), assemblies, (.IAM) and drawings (.IDW or .DWG) that are associated with the project. The operation does not add files that are already in the vault.

To add Autodesk Inventor project files to the vault, they must be Vault projects and the project folders must be mapped to vault folders.

- The *OldVersions* folder and its contents, lock files (.LCK), and other project files in the active project, are not added.

How To: Bulk Load Multiple Designs

1. In the Application Menu, expand Vault Server and select **Check In Project**. A scan is performed on the project files to find files that are not currently in the vault. Files not found in the vault are listed in the Check In Project dialog box.
2. In the *Enter comments to include...* area, enter comments as required.
3. Click **OK** to add all of the files to the vault. If you need to remove the files from the local directories after they have been loaded into the vault, you must remove them manually.

Autoloader

Autodesk Autoloader for Vault is a utility that is provided with the Autodesk Vault installation kit. It includes tools to assist with gathering, analyzing, and loading Autodesk Inventor designs into the vault. This utility is used outside the Autodesk Inventor software. During the analysis or scanning phase, you are informed of any issues (such as missing references and duplicate files) so they can be addressed before the files are loaded into the vault. The Autodesk Autoloader for Vault is recommended when bulk loading large Autodesk Inventor projects. It can also upload legacy projects.

Add Library Files

Library files can also be added to the vault using the **Check In** and **Check In Project** operations. Library files can be added if the library path in the project file is mapped to a vault folder. Library files are the only files located outside the workspace that are added to the vault using the **Check In Project** option.

Categories

Categories enable you to group objects and assign a defined set of behaviors and rules to objects. For example, a category can automatically assign user-defined properties to objects in the Vault, automatically assign lifecycle definitions, or automatically set revision values to files.

How To: Change a Category

1. Select an object and then select **Change Category** from the toolbar or from the **Actions** menu.
2. Select a new category from the drop-down list, as shown in Figure 3–24.

You can also change the category of a file from the Vault Browser shortcut menu.

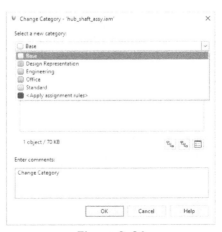

Figure 3–24

3. Click **OK**.

Practice 3a	# Creating a Vault Project

Practice Objective

- Create a vault project and map folders.

In this practice, you will set up a vault master project for the database and map the folders.

Task 1 - Create a vault project.

In this task, you will create a vault master project file to use for all vault designs.

1. Launch the Autodesk Inventor software.

2. In the *Get Started* tab>Launch panel, click 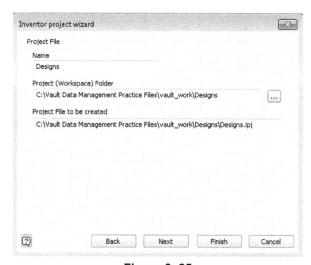 (Projects).

3. Click **New** to create a new project file.

4. Select **New Vault Project** and click **Next**.

5. For *Name*, type **Designs**. Set the *Project (Workspace) Folder* to *C:\Vault Data Management Practice Files\vault_work\ Designs*, as shown in Figure 3–25.

Inventor project wizard

Project File
Name
Designs

Project (Workspace) Folder
C:\Vault Data Management Practice Files\vault_work\Designs

Project File to be created
C:\Vault Data Management Practice Files\vault_work\Designs\Designs.ipj

Back   Next   Finish   Cancel

Figure 3–25

6. Click **Finish**.

7. In the Projects dialog box, double-click on the Designs project name to make the new project active. A checkmark displays next to the project name to indicate that it is the active project.

8. In the *Project Details* area, expand Folder Options. Right-click on Content Center Files and select **Edit**. Browse to the directory path shown in Figure 3–26. Click **OK** and press <Enter>.

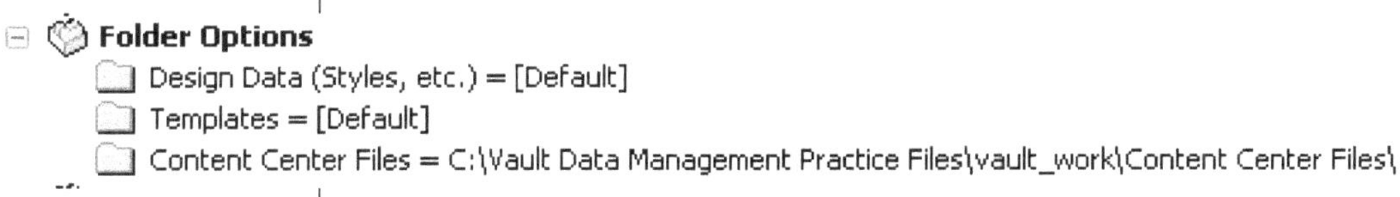

⊟ 🛇 **Folder Options**
　　📁 Design Data (Styles, etc.) = [Default]
　　📁 Templates = [Default]
　　📁 Content Center Files = C:\Vault Data Management Practice Files\vault_work\Content Center Files\

Figure 3–26

9. Click **Save** to save the changes.

10. Click **Done** to complete the creation of the master vault project that can be used for all vault designs.

Task 2 - Map folders.

In this task, you will map the local folders (i.e., the active project's workspace) to the vault folders so that Autodesk Inventor files can be added to and accessed from the vault. This operation only needs to be performed once.

1. In the *Vault* tab>Access panel, click 🔲 (Log In). Log in as **user1**, no password, to the *Vault_Training* vault. If **Log In** is grayed out, you are already logged into the vault. Log out and log back in again to ensure that you are logged in to the correct User Name and Vault.

2. In the *Vault* tab, expand the Access panel, and click 🔲 (Connection Status) to verify your login and vault information. Click **OK**.

3. In the *Vault* tab, expand the Access panel again, and click 🔲 (Map folders) to map the newly created master vault project to vault folders.

4. In the Project Folder Mapping dialog box (as shown in Figure 3–27) you will map the Project Root and Content Center Files directories to specific folders in the vault. Select **Project Root** and click **Edit...**.

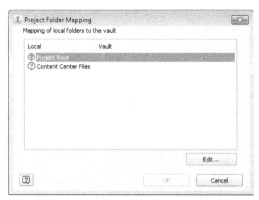

Figure 3–27

5. The Browse Vault For Folder dialog box opens listing the folders that are currently in the vault.

6. Select the *Designs* subfolder and click **OK**.

7. In the Project Folder Mapping dialog box, select **Content Center Files** and click **Edit...**.

8. Select the *Content Center Files* subfolder and click **OK**. The Project Folder Mapping dialog box updates as shown in Figure 3–28.

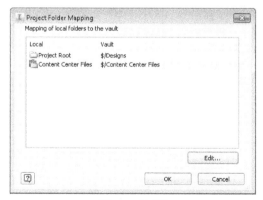

Figure 3–28

9. Click **OK** to complete the mapping changes and close the Project Folder Mapping dialog box. The vault folders are now mapped for your master project workspace.

Practice 3b

Using Open From Vault and Vault Browser

Practice Objectives

- Open a file from the vault from in the Autodesk Inventor software.
- Use the Vault Browser to check in a project file to the vault.
- Display the history of a design file in Vault Browser.

In this practice, you will log in to the vault from the Autodesk Inventor software, check in a project file to the vault, open an assembly file, and display the history of the assembly's design.

Task 1 - Open a file from the vault.

In this task, you will open an Autodesk Inventor file directly from the vault using the **Open** option in the *Vault* tab>Access panel in the Autodesk Inventor software.

1. In the Autodesk Inventor software, in the *Vault* tab>Access panel, click ![icon] (Open).

2. In the $\Designs\Hub Shaft* folder, select **hub_shaft_assy.iam** as shown in Figure 3–29.

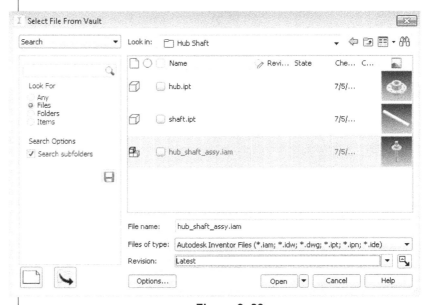

Figure 3–29

3. Click **Open**.

4. Click **No** if prompted to check out the assembly. A read-only copy of the file opens.

Task 2 - Use the Vault Browser.

In this task, you will use the Vault Browser to view the vault status of the listed Autodesk Inventor files.

1. In the Browser Panel, select **Vault**, as shown in Figure 3–30, to open the Vault Browser.

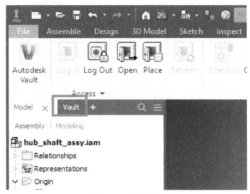

Figure 3–30

2. A circle with a plus sign (⊕) displays next to the **Designs.ipj** project file, as shown in Figure 3–31. Move the cursor over the project file to display the tooltip indicating that it is not in the vault. All of the other files display an empty white circle, indicating that the version of the file copied to the working folder that you are working on is the same as the one in the vault, also known as the *Latest Version*.

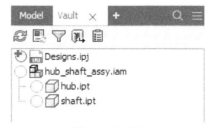

Figure 3–31

Task 3 - Check in a project file to the vault.

In this task, you will add the project file to the vault as required, which will change the vault status icon.

1. In the Vault Browser, select **Designs.ipj**, right-click, and select **Check In**, as shown in Figure 3–32.

Figure 3–32

2. In the Check In dialog box, in the *Enter comments to include...* area, type **Initial submission**.

3. Click **OK** to finish adding the file to the vault. The vault status icon is now the same as that of the other files.

Task 4 - Display the history of the file.

In this task, you will view the history of the Autodesk Inventor design in the Vault Browser.

1. In the Vault Browser, select **hub_shaft_assy.iam**, right-click, and select **Show Details...**. If required, select the **Show all versions** checkbox. The Details window displays the five versions currently in the vault, as shown in Figure 3–33.

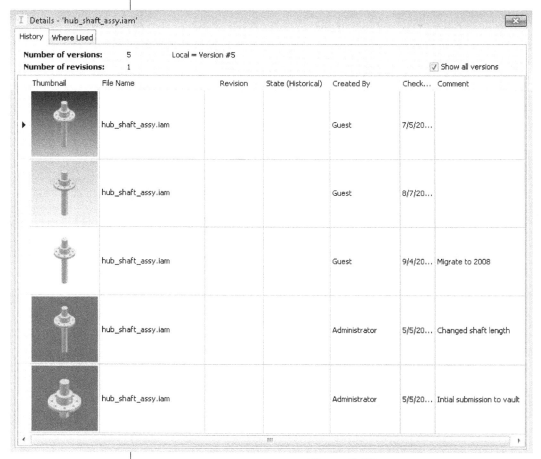

Figure 3–33

2. Close the Details window.

3. Close **hub_shaft_assy.iam**.

Practice 3c

Adding an Autodesk Inventor Design to the Vault

Practice Objectives

- Use the **Check In** command to add an Autodesk Inventor design to the vault.
- Verify the added files in the Autodesk Vault software.

In this practice, you will add an Autodesk Inventor assembly to the vault using the **Check In** command, and then view its design files in Autodesk Vault.

Task 1 - Retrieve an assembly.

In this task, you will retrieve an Autodesk Inventor assembly from a local directory that is not already in the vault.

1. In the *Get Started* tab>Launch panel, click 📂 (Open). In the *Top Plate* folder, select **topplate Assy.iam** and open the assembly in the Autodesk Inventor software.

2. Open the Vault Browser. The files display circles with plus signs indicating that they have not been added to the vault, as shown in Figure 3–34.

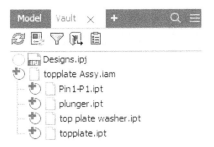

Figure 3–34

Task 2 - Use the Check In command.

In this task, you will add the Autodesk Inventor assembly to the vault using the Vault Browser.

1. In the Vault Browser, select **topplate Assy.iam**, right-click, and select **Check In**.

2. The Check In dialog box opens displaying all of the files to be added to the vault, including the folder structure that will be created, as shown in Figure 3–35. Ensure that the **Keep files checked out** option is not selected.

Figure 3–35

3. Note at the top of the dialog box. It indicates that the **Create visualization attachment** option is disabled. Click **Settings**. Select **Create visualization attachment** and **Apply to all files**, as shown in Figure 3–36.

Figure 3–36

4. Click **OK**.

5. In the *Enter comments to include...* area, type **Initial Submission**.

6. Click **OK** to add the files to the vault.

7. Close **topplate Assy.iam**.

Task 3 - Verify the files in the vault.

In this task, you will use the Autodesk Vault software to verify that the Autodesk Inventor design files have been added to the vault and that the relationships have been maintained.

1. In the *Vault* tab>Access panel, click (Autodesk Vault) to launch the Autodesk Vault software if it was closed.

2. Click (Refresh) to update the vault status icons.

3. In the Navigation pane, expand the $\Designs* folder structure and select the *Top Plate* folder to view the files have just been added to the vault, as shown in Figure 3–37. The *Top Plate* folder was automatically created when the design files were added.

Figure 3–37

4. Select **plunger.ipt** in the Main table.

5. In the Preview pane, select the *History* tab. The file displays Version 1 because it was just added by user1, as shown in Figure 3–38. All of the other files that were checked in as part of the topplate **Assy.iam** file are also version 1.

Figure 3–38

6. Select the *Preview* tab and select the **Version 1** thumbnail. The model displays because the .DWF was created when the files were added to the vault.

7. In the Preview pane, select the *Where Used* tab and then expand **plunger.ipt** to view the relationships between the files, as shown in Figure 3–39.

Figure 3–39

8. In the Main table, select **topplate Assy.iam** and select the *Uses* tab to view the files used by the assembly, as shown in Figure 3–40.

Figure 3–40

9. Close **topplate Assy.asm**.

Practice 3d

Bulk Loading Autodesk Inventor Files into the Vault

Practice Objective

- Use the Check In Project command to bulk load multiple design projects into the vault.

In this practice, you will use the **Check In Project** operation to bulk load multiple design projects into the vault. You will then verify the results of the bulk loading and change the category on some of the design files.

Task 1 - View design files in the working folder and add them to the vault.

In this task, you will open the working folder to view the design files and then use the **Check In Project** operation to add them to the vault.

1. In the Autodesk Inventor software, in the *Vault* tab, expand the Access panel, and click 🗀 (Go to Workspace). A Windows Explorer window opens displaying the workspace folder structure.

2. Compare this folder structure to the *Designs* folder structure in the Autodesk Vault software. The designs: *Arm System*, *Mold Assembly*, *Piston*, *Vise*, and *Yoke* have not been added to the vault.

3. In the Autodesk Inventor software, select **File>Vault Server**, and then hover the cursor over ▼ at the bottom of the menu to scroll down. Click 🗗 (Check In Project) to bulk load these designs into the vault. All of the files in the selected folder are bulk loaded.

4. In the Check In Project dialog box, in the *Enter comments to include...* area, type **Initial Submission** and click **OK**.

5. Close the Autodesk Inventor software.

Task 2 - Verify the results in the Autodesk Vault software.

In this task, you will verify that the new Autodesk Inventor designs have been added to the vault successfully using the **Check In Project** operation.

1. In the Autodesk Vault software, click 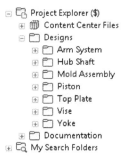 (Refresh) and expand the $\Designs folder to verify that the bulk upload process has added the new design folders and all of their design files as shown in Figure 3–41.

Figure 3–41

Task 3 - Remove the files from Windows Explorer.

Now that the files have been loaded into the vault, you will remove all of the *Design* folders (including their contents) from the local working directory, with the exception of the **Designs.ipj** project file. This is a recommended best practice to ensure that you are always using the latest version of the files from the vault.

1. In the Vault, select the ...\Designs folder, right-click and select **Go To Working Folder**. Remove the folders and their contents from Windows Explorer, keeping only **Designs.ipj**.

2. Close Windows Explorer.

Task 4 - Change the Category to Engineering.

In this task, you will change the category to Engineering for the Vise design files.

1. In the Autodesk Vault software, in the %\Designs\Vise folder, use <Ctrl>+<A> to select all of the files and then click **Change Category** on the toolbar.

2. Select **Engineering** from the Select a new category drop-down list, as shown in Figure 3–42.

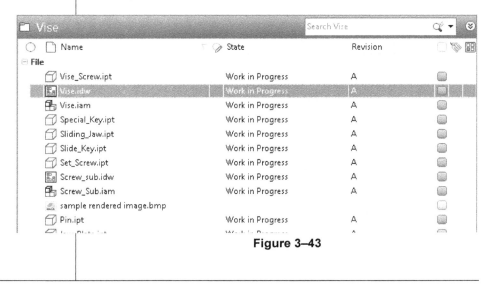

Figure 3–42

3. Click **OK**.

4. Note that the files in the *Vise* folder are now updated with the **Engineering** category and display **Revision A**, as shown in Figure 3–43.

	Name	State	Revision		
⊟ **File**					
	Vise_Screw.ipt	Work in Progress	A		
	Vise.idw	Work in Progress	A		
	Vise.iam	Work in Progress	A		
	Special_Key.ipt	Work in Progress	A		
	Sliding_Jaw.ipt	Work in Progress	A		
	Slide_Key.ipt	Work in Progress	A		
	Set_Screw.ipt	Work in Progress	A		
	Screw_sub.idw	Work in Progress	A		
	Screw_Sub.iam	Work in Progress	A		
	sample rendered image.bmp				
	Pin.ipt	Work in Progress	A		

Figure 3–43

Task 5 - Change category on Piston design files.

In this task, you will perform the same change category operation, this time on the Piston design files.

1. In the Autodesk Vault software, in the %*Designs\Piston* folder, use <Ctrl>+<A> to select all of the files and then click **Change Category** on the toolbar.

2. Select the **Engineering** category for all of the Piston design files.

3. Click **OK**.

Chapter Review Questions

1. What is true of the single vault project method? (Select all that apply.)

   a. All projects or designs reference the one master project file.

   b. Not recommended by Autodesk.

   c. The simplest and most robust way of setting up your Autodesk Inventor Vault integration.

   d. All of the above.

2. In Figure 3–44, the highlighted Open icon retrieves files from the local workspace and not from the vault.

   a. True

   b. False

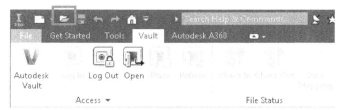

Figure 3–44

3. In the Autodesk Inventor software, which operation enables you to associate the local folder structure to the corresponding folder structure in the vault so that Autodesk Inventor files can be added and/or accessed?

   a. Place from Vault

   b. Check In Project

   c. Open from Vault

   d. Map Folders

4. You can use the **Open (Read Only)** option in the Open drop-down list if you only want to view an Autodesk Inventor file and not make changes.

   a. True

   b. False

5. In the Vault Browser, what could the reason be when a filename displays with a white circle and a plus sign?

   a. The files are not yet in the vault.

   b. You are not working on the Latest Version.

   c. The file is not available for **Check Out**.

   d. All of the above.

6. How can Autodesk Inventor files be added to the vault for the first time to ensure all file relationships stay intact? (Select all that apply.)

   a. In the Autodesk Inventor software, use the **Check In** command.

   b. In the Autodesk Vault client software, use the **Check In** command.

   c. In the Autodesk Inventor software, use the **Check In Project** command.

   d. Use the Autodesk Autoloader utility.

Command Summary

Button	Command	Location
	Log In	• **Autodesk Inventor Ribbon:** *Vault* tab>Access panel
	Map Folders	• **Autodesk Inventor Ribbon:** *Vault* tab>Access panel
	Open	• **Autodesk Inventor Quick Access Toolbar**
	Open	• **Autodesk Inventor Ribbon:** *Vault* tab>Access panel
	Options	• **Autodesk Inventor Ribbon:** *Vault* tab>File Status panel
	Place	• **Autodesk Inventor Ribbon:** *Vault* tab>Access panel
	Projects	• **Autodesk Inventor Ribbon:** *Get Started* tab>Launch panel

Chapter 4

Searching the Vault

The Autodesk® Vault software provides a variety of search methods to locate files in the database. You can use a basic text string search or an advanced search on one or more file properties. Vaults can also be configured by the Administrator to perform a full content search of known file formats. Specialized searches enable you to easily locate specific objects in a large database.

Learning Objectives in this Chapter

- Search for files in the Autodesk Vault software using the search methods of Browsing folders, Quick Search, Basic Find, and Advanced Find.
- Differentiate between search methods
- Create a saved search, edit a saved search, and run a saved search.
- Manage saved searches using Rename, Copy and Delete operations.
- Create a search report.

4.1 Overview of Search Methods

Locating a file quickly and easily becomes important when design projects and databases contain a large number of files. Since Vault stores file properties and indexes them in the database, they can quickly be queried to locate a particular file.

Use this table to compare search methods and decide which method best suits your needs.

Four main search operations enable you to locate files in the database: **Browse Folders**, **Quick Search**, **Basic Find**, and **Advanced Find**.

Search Tool	Description
Browse Folders	Enables you to navigate the folder structure in the Navigation pane to find and view design folders and files. Click ⊞ (Expand) to expand the folder structure and ⊟ (Collapse) to collapse it (similar to Windows Explorer).

	⊟ 🗂 Project Explorer ($)
	   ⊞ 🗂 Content Center Files
	   ⊟ 🗂 Designs
	     ⊞ 🗂 Arm System
	     ⊞ 🗂 Hub Shaft
	     ⊞ 🗂 Mold Assembly
	     ⊞ 🗂 Piston
	     ⊞ 🗂 Top Plate
	     ⊞ 🗂 Vise
	     ⊞ 🗂 Yoke
	   ⊞ 🗂 Documentation
	  ⊞ 🗂 My Search Folders

Quick Search	The Quick Search is located in the Main table title bar. Quick Search enables you to search on all of the file properties in the folders based on a specified text string.
	You can also click ⊗ (Expand the query builder) to set specific property search criteria and ▾ (Show search options menu) to access additional search options.

Basic Find	The Basic Find is located in the Find dialog box and enables you to search by entering a specified text string. The search locates any file or object in the vault that contains the search string in any of the file properties.

Look For: Look In:

Any ▼   Vault_Training - user 1

Basic | Advanced | Options

Search for:
Search Text:

☐ Search file content

Advanced Find	The Advanced Find is located in the Find dialog box and enables you to create advanced searches by specifying file property criteria. The search locates the files and objects that match that criteria.

Look For: Look In:

Any ▼   Vault_Training - user 1

Basic   Advanced | Options

Search for:
Property: Condition: Value:

▼

Searches defined using Quick Search or the Find dialog box (**Basic** or **Advanced**) can be saved to be used again. For quick access, any saved search can be added to *My Search Folders* in the Navigation pane. You can also select the saved search from the Open From Vault and Place From Vault dialog boxes in the Autodesk Inventor software.

Wildcard and Boolean Operators

Wildcards and Boolean operators can be used in **Basic** and **Advanced Find** operations.

Wildcard Operators

Wildcard	Description
*	Represents any characters.
?	Represents a single character.

Boolean Operators (case insensitive)

Operator	Description
and	Search results return anything containing both words.
or	Search results return anything containing either word.
not	The search results exclude anything containing the specified word.
" "	The search results return everything containing the exact phrase in the quotes.

4.2 Browsing Folder Structure

In the Autodesk Vault software, you can browse the created folder structure to search for files. This is useful when you know the folder or design name and want to view its associated files.

To browse, click ⊞ (Expand) to display the expanded folder structure. When the design folder is found and selected, its associated files display in the Main pane on the right side. An example of a selected design file is shown in Figure 4–1.

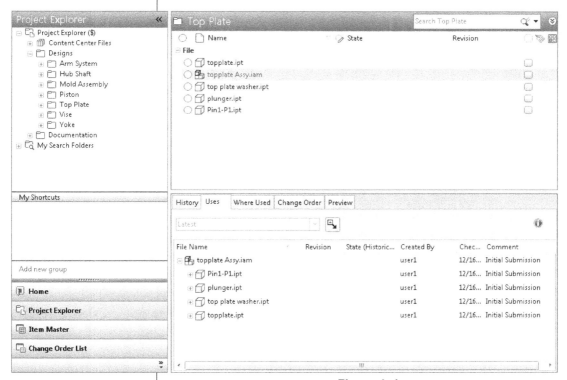

Figure 4–1

4.3 Quick Search

The **Quick Search** performs a search on all of the file properties in the folders based on the specified text string. **Quick Search** is located in the Main table's title bar, as shown in Figure 4–2.

Figure 4–2

How To: Perform a Quick Search

1. In the *Search* field, enter a text string.

2. Click ⚲ (Search) or press <Enter>. The search results display.

3. Click ˣ (Clear or cancel search) to return to the contents of the main table.

Recent Searches

To access a list of recent searches, click ˅ (Show search options menu) and select **Recent Searches**. Select a recent search (as shown in Figure 4–3) to execute the search.

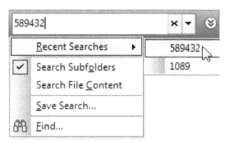

Figure 4–3

Query Builder

To specify additional criteria for your search, click 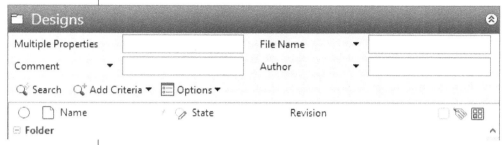 (Expand the query builder) in the title bar to expand the Query Builder, as shown in Figure 4–4.

Figure 4–4

How To: Add Search Criteria using Query Builder

1. Click 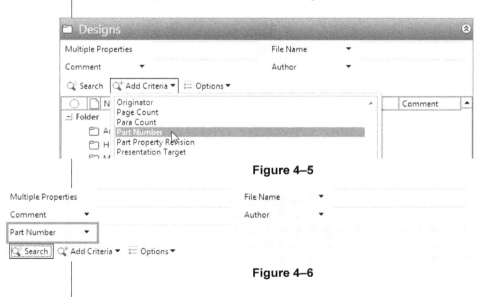 to expand the Query Builder.
2. In the *Multiple Properties* field, enter the value that you want to search for in the properties.
3. If required, enter values in the *File Name*, *Comment,* and *Author* fields.

The Query Builder properties selected are kept from session to session.

4. To add a search for a specific property, click **Add Criteria** and select the property. For example, the **Part Number** property is selected as shown in Figure 4–5, and added as a property to search as shown in Figure 4–6.

Figure 4–5

Figure 4–6

5. You can also change an existing property to another property or delete a property by clicking the down arrow next to the property name, as shown in Figure 4–7.

Figure 4–7

6. Click **Search** to execute the search and display the search results.

4.4 Basic Find

The **Basic Find** performs a search on all file properties in the folders based on the specified text string. You can access the **Basic Find** functionality in the *Basic* tab in the Find dialog box. Click **Find...** in the Standard toolbar to open the Find dialog box. You can also open the Find dialog box by selecting **Tools>Find** or pressing <Ctrl>+<F>. The Find dialog box opens as shown in Figure 4–8.

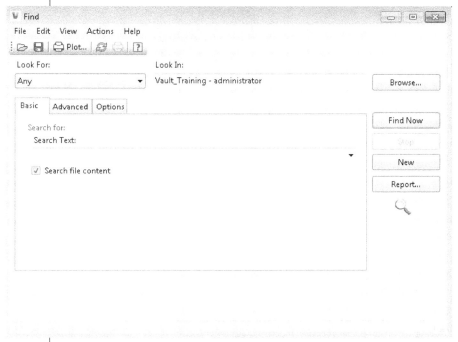

Figure 4–8

Specify which folders to search by clicking **Browse...** next to *Look In*. Select **Search file content** to search the contents of files. The Content Indexing Service must be enabled in the Autodesk Vault Manager to perform a full content search.

How To: Perform a Basic Find

1. In the Find dialog box, select the *Basic* tab.
2. For *Look In*, browse to the vault folder that you want to search. By default, the entire vault is searched. To refine the search, click **Browse...** and select the folders to be searched. To search the contents of the files, select **Search file content**.
3. Enter the required keywords, including any wildcards or boolean operators to help define the search.
4. Select the *Options* tab to confirm or clear the optional settings shown in Figure 4–9.

The Search Text drop-down list stores the 10 most recent searches.

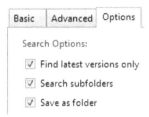

Figure 4–9

5. Press <Enter> or click **Find Now** to execute the search.
6. The search results display at the bottom of the Find dialog box, in which you can sort or customize the columns. You can perform actions on the resulting files by right-clicking and selecting an option.
7. Click **New** if you want to define a new search.

*You can also expand **Actions** and select an option to modify the files.*

4.5 Advanced Find

An **Advanced Find** provides greater flexibility over the search criteria. In the *Advanced* tab in the Find dialog box, you can define more in-depth search criteria using *Property*, *Condition*, and *Value*, as shown in Figure 4–10.

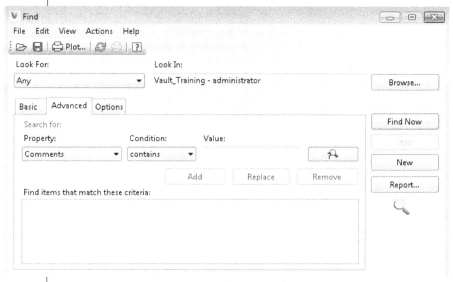

Figure 4–10

How To: Perform an Advanced Find

1. In the Find dialog box, select the *Advanced* tab.
2. For *Look In*, browse to the vault folder that you want to search. By default, the entire vault is searched. Click **Browse...** to refine the search by selecting specific folders.
3. Expand the Property drop-down list and select an option.
4. Expand the Condition drop-down list and select an option. The conditions for a text field are shown in Figure 4–11.

Custom properties are also available for searching.

Figure 4–11

5. The options available in the drop-down list depend on the type of Property selected. For example, the Conditions for a date field include: **is**, **before**, **after**, **on or before**, **on or after**, **Yesterday**, **Today**, **Tomorrow**, **Last # Days**, **Next # Days**, **Last Week**, **This Week**, and **Next Week**, while those for a numeric field include: **is**, **<=**, **<**, **>=**, **>**, and **is not**.

6. In the *Value* field, enter the value for the condition.

7. Click **Add** to add the properties to the list of criteria.

8. Repeat Steps 3 to 6 to add more properties to refine the search results.

9. If you need to remove any of the search criteria, select them in the *Find items that match these criteria* field and click **Remove**.

10. Select the *Options* tab to confirm or clear the optional settings shown in Figure 4–12.

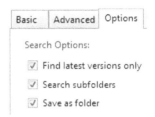

Figure 4–12

11. When the search criteria and settings have been defined, click **Find Now** to execute the search.

You can also expand Actions and select an option to modify the files.

12. The search results display at the bottom of the dialog box. You can sort or customize the columns, and perform actions on the files by right-clicking and selecting an option.

13. Click **New** to define a new search.

4.6 Saving Searches

Once you have defined a search, you can save the search criteria so that you can perform the same search again. In addition to defining and saving searches, the Find dialog box enables you to open and manage saved searches.

How To: Save a Search for Reuse

You can also click

 *(Save Current Search) in the Find toolbar.*

1. In the Find dialog box, select **File>Save Search** when your search results display.
2. For *Search Name*, type a name for the saved search in the Save Search dialog box, as shown in Figure 4–13.

Figure 4–13

3. By default, the **Save As Folder** option is selected. It saves the search as a folder in the *My Search Folders* area so that it can be quickly accessed later.
4. Click **OK** to finish saving the search.

Save A Quick Searches

To save a Quick Search, click ˅ (Show search options menu) and select **Save Search** as shown in Figure 4–14.

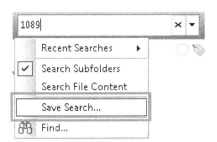

Figure 4–14

Save a Query Builder Search

To save a search from Query Builder, click **Options** and select **Save Search**, as shown in Figure 4–15.

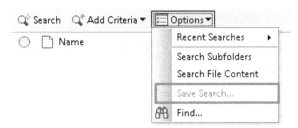

Figure 4–15

My Search Folders

Searches saved with the **Save As Folder** option selected display in the *My Search Folders* area in the Navigation pane in the Autodesk Vault software, as shown in Figure 4–16.

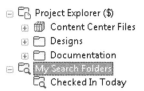

Figure 4–16

To display a search, select the required search folder name in the *My Search Folders* area. The results display in the Main table. A **Find** can also be performed on a search folder to narrow the results.

Run a Saved Search

You can use the Open Saved Search dialog box to run searches that were not saved in the *My Search Folders* area. Select **File>Open Search** in the Find dialog box and then select a saved search in the Open Saved Search dialog box, as shown in Figure 4–17.

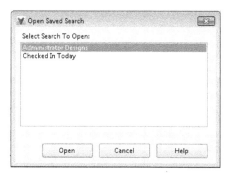

Figure 4–17

How To: Run a Saved Search

1. In the Find dialog box, select **File>Open Search**.
2. In the Open Saved Search dialog box, select the saved search from the list.
3. Click **Open** to execute the search. The search results display in the Find dialog box. The dialog box switches to the tab in which the save was created: *Basic* or *Advanced*.

You can also click

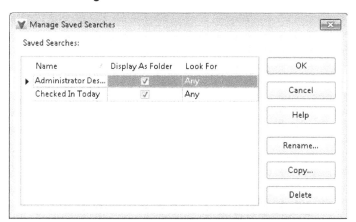 *(Open Search) in the toolbar.*

Manage Saved Searches

You can organize your saved searches in the Manage Saved Searches dialog box. You can rename, copy, and delete saved searches. You can also control whether the saved search displays as a folder in the *My Saved Searches* area.

How To: Modify a Saved Search

1. In the Find dialog box, select **File>Manage Saved Searches**. The Manage Saved Searches dialog box opens as shown in Figure 4–18.

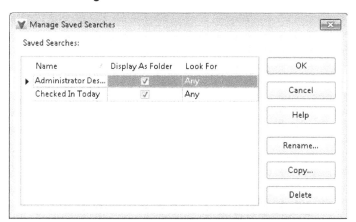

Figure 4–18

*If a search is saved as a search folder, you can also rename the search in the Search Folder list in the Navigation pane by right-clicking and selecting **Rename**.*

2. Perform the following tasks as required:
   - To rename a search, select the search name and click **Rename...**. Enter the new name in the Rename Search dialog box and click **OK**.
   - To copy a search, select the search name in the Manage Saved Searches dialog box and click **Copy...**. Enter the new name and click **OK**.
   - To remove the search from the *My Search Folders* area, clear the **Display As Folder** option.
3. Click **OK** to save the changes and close the Manage Saved Searches dialog box.

Edit Search

You can edit the saved search criteria in the Find dialog box or *My Search Folders* area.

How To: Edit a Saved Search from the Find Dialog Box

1. In the Find dialog box, select **File>Open Search**.
2. In the Open Saved Search dialog box, select the saved search from the list.
3. Click **Open** and make your changes.
4. Click 🖫 (Save Current Search) to save the search with your changes.

How To: Edit a Saved Search from *My Search Folders* Area

1. In *My Search Folders* area, right-click on your saved search and select **Edit Saved Search**, as shown in Figure 4–19.

Figure 4–19

2. The Find dialog box opens with the saved search selected.
3. Make the required changes and click 🖫 (Save Current Search) to save the search with the changes.

Deleting a Saved Search

If a search is saved as a search folder, you can delete the search from the *My Search Folder* area in the Navigation pane or in the Manage Saved Searches dialog box. You are prompted to confirm the deletion of the selected saved search.

How To: Delete a Saved Search

*In the My Search Folder area, right-click and select **Delete**.*

1. In the Find dialog box, select **File>Manage Saved Searches**.
2. In the Manage Saved Searches dialog box, select the search that you want to delete.
3. Click **Delete**.
4. In the Warning box, click **Yes** to confirm the deletion.
5. In the Manage Saved Searches dialog box, click **OK** to save the changes and close the Manage Saved Searches dialog box.

4.7 Reports

There are a number of default report templates available in the Autodesk Vault software. You can use these templates to create Reports. The following lists a few ways to access the Report functionality.

- In the Find dialog box, when Search Results display, click **Report**, as shown in Figure 4–20.

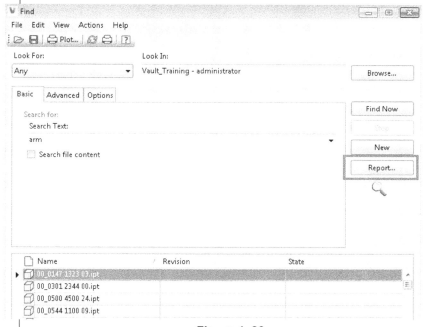

Figure 4–20

- With a folder selected in the Navigation pane, click **Report** on the toolbar, as shown in Figure 4–21. You can also use this button if the folder is selected in the Main table.

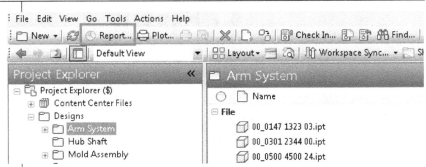

Figure 4–21

- In the My Search Folders, right-click on a saved search and select **Report**, as shown in Figure 4–22.

Figure 4–22

Practice 4a

Searches

Practice Objective

- Search using a **Basic Find**, **Quick Search**, and **Advanced Find** operation.

In this practice you will run a variety of searches, including Basic Find, Quick Search, and Advanced Find, to locate files in the database. Each search will produce a view of the database that contains the files that meet the search criteria. You will also use different methods of verifying the search results and search the file contents.

Task 1 - Search using the Basic Find tab.

In this task, you will locate all of the files in the $\Designs$ folder that contain the word *arm* in their file properties.

1. In the Autodesk Vault software, click **Find** to open the Find dialog box.

2. Select the *Basic* tab.

3. In the *Search Text* field, type **arm*** as shown in Figure 4–23. Select **Search file content**.

*The **Basic Find** searches the File Name field. To simplify the search, you can clear the **Search file content** option if you know that you are looking for the search string text in the File Name.*

Figure 4–23

4. Click **Find Now**. The search results display as shown in Figure 4–24. Some of the files display the word *arm* in their filenames. However, **3136 1149 25.iam** does not.

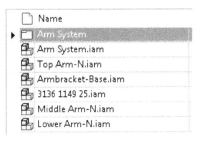

Figure 4–24

---

5. To determine which file property in **3136 1149 25.iam** contains the word *arm* and to verify the search results, select the file, right-click, and select **Go to Folder**.

6. Note that *Description* contains the text: **Armbracket**, as shown in Figure 4–25. This verifies that the word **arm** was found in the Description file property.

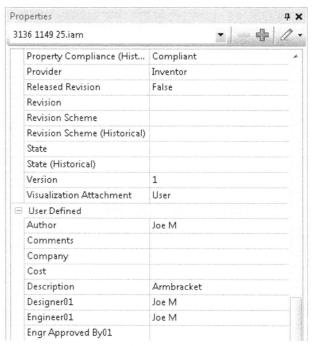

Properties	⚐ ✕
3136 1149 25.iam	▼ ╬ ✎ ▼
Property Compliance (Hist...	Compliant
Provider	Inventor
Released Revision	False
Revision	
Revision Scheme	
Revision Scheme (Historical)	
State	
State (Historical)	
Version	1
Visualization Attachment	User
⊟ User Defined	
Author	Joe M
Comments	
Company	
Cost	
Description	Armbracket
Designer01	Joe M
Engineer01	Joe M
Engr Approved By01	

Figure 4–25

7. Close the Find dialog box.

Task 2 - Search using Quick Search.

In this task, you will also search for the keyword **arm*** but this time using the Quick Search.

1. In the *Designs* folder, in the Search field, type **arm*** as shown in Figure 4–26.

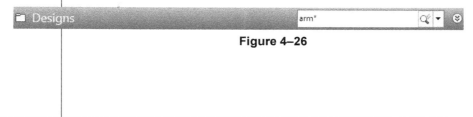

📁 Designs   arm*   🔍 ▼ ⊗

Figure 4–26

2. Click ⚲ (Search). The search results display and are the same as in Task 1.

Task 3 - Search using the Advanced Find tab.

In this task, you will find all of the files in the vault in which the file property called *Designer01* has the value of **Administrator**. You will first run a **Basic Find** with the keyword **Administrator** to display its results. You will then run the search again using the **Advanced Find** search and compare the results to identify the benefits of using each method.

1. Click **Find**. In the Find dialog box, in the *Basic* tab, in the *Search Text* field, type **Administrator**.

2. Click **Find Now** to execute the search.

3. The search results include all of the files that have been created by the Administrator user and any files that contain the string *Administrator* as a property. Since you only want to display files in which the Designer01 file property is *Administrator*, you need to use the **Advanced Find**.

4. Select the *Advanced* tab.

5. Set the *Property* to **Designer01**, set the *Condition* to **is**, and set the *Value* to **Administrator**.

6. Click **Add** to add the criteria.

7. Click **Find Now** to execute the search. The search results list only displays **yoke.ipt** this time.

8. To verify the results, select **yoke.ipt**, right-click, and select **Go to Folder.**

9. In the Properties grid, scroll down and note that the *Designer01* user-defined property contains the text: **Administrator**, as shown in Figure 4–27.

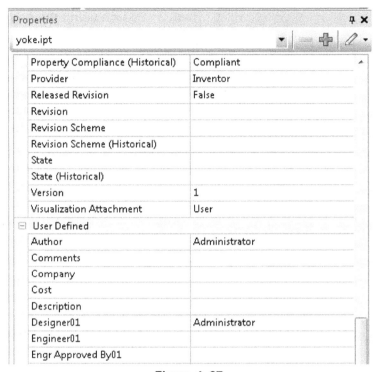

Figure 4–27.

10. Leave the Find dialog box open.

Task 4 - Perform another Advanced Find.

In this task, you will find all assemblies that use a specific library part. You are provided with a portion of the description for the library part *hex bolt*. However, you do not know the filename.

1. In the Find dialog box, click **New** to start a new search.

2. Set the *Property* to **Description**, set the *Condition* to **contains**, and set the *Value* to **hex bolt**.

3. Click **Add** to add the criteria.

4. Click **Find Now** to execute the search. The search results display one result: **local.ANSI.62.230.1.ipt**.

5. Select the library part in the results list, right-click, and select **Go To Folder**. Autodesk Vault displays the vault folder in which the library part is located (*Mold Assembly* folder).

6. Close the Find dialog box.

7. Select **local.ANSI.62.230.1.ipt**. In the Preview pane, select the *Where Used* tab. Note that the part is used in **Final Mold Assy.iam**, as shown in Figure 4–28.

Figure 4–28.

Practice 4b

Saved Searches

Practice Objectives

- Save a search
- Run a Saved Search.
- Run a Search Report.
- Modify a Saved Search.
- Delete a Saved Search.
- Save a Search in My Search Folders.

In this practice, you will create several saved searches so that you can run them later for quick access to files that meet the search criteria. You will also modify a saved search, save a search in My Search Folders, and delete a saved search.

Task 1 - Save a search.

In this task, you will create and save a search that locates all of the Autodesk Inventor assemblies in the vault.

1. Open the Find dialog box and select the *Advanced* tab.

2. In the *Search for* area, add the following criteria: **File Extension**, **contains**, and **iam**. Click **Add** to add the criteria. Run the search.

3. In the Find dialog box, select **File>Save Search**. Your search is saved in the following location:
   - *C:\Users\[Username]\AppData\Roaming\Autodesk\ VaultCommon\Servers\Services_Security_*\localhost\ Vaults\[Vault_name]\Searches*

4. For the *Search Name*, type **All Assemblies**.

5. Clear the **Save As Folder** option and click **OK**.

6. Click **New** to clear the search and its results.

Task 2 - Run a saved search.

In this task, you will run the **All Assemblies** saved search.

1. In the Find dialog box, select **File>Open Search**.

2. Select **All Assemblies** and click **Open** to run the search.

Task 3 - Run a Search Report.

In this task, you will run a search report.

1. In the Find dialog box, click **Report**, as shown in Figure 4–29.

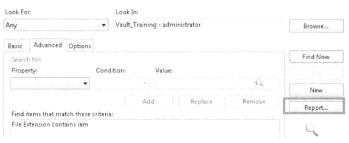

Figure 4–29

2. Select **File Detail.rdlc**, as shown in Figure 4–30.

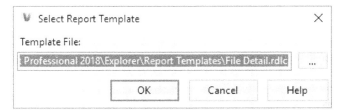

Figure 4–30

3. Click **OK**. The report will display as shown in Figure 4–31.

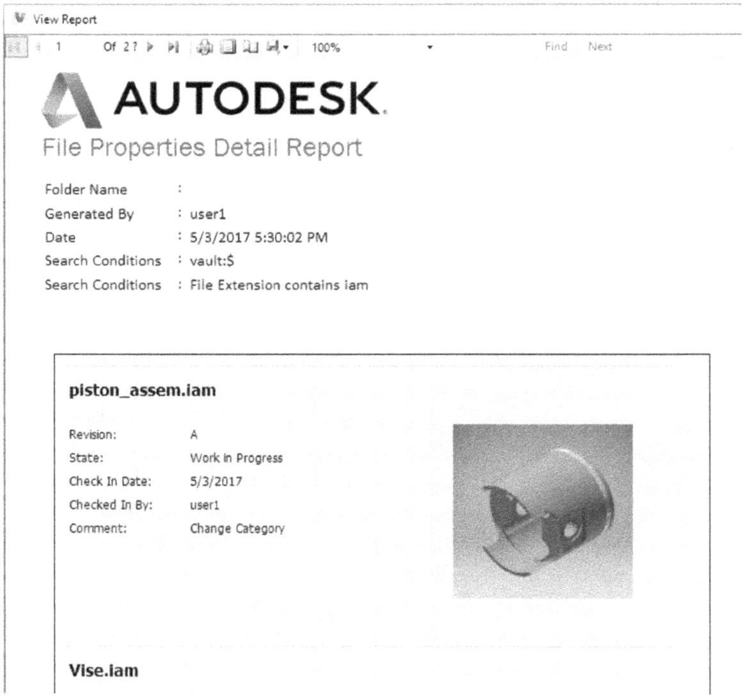

Figure 4–31

4. Close the report.

Task 4 - Modify a saved search.

In this task, you will modify the **All Assemblies** saved search to display as a search folder and rename it **All Assembly Models**.

1. In the Find dialog box, select **File>Manage Saved Searches**.

2. In the Manage Saved Searches dialog box, select the **All Assemblies** search and click **Rename...**.

3. For the *Search Name*, type **All Assembly Models** as the new name and click **OK**.

4. In the Manage Saved Searches dialog box, select **Display As Folder**.

5. Click **OK** to save the changes. The *All Assembly Models* search folder displays in the Navigation pane, in the *My Search Folders* area, as shown in Figure 4–32.

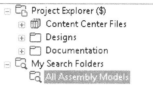

Figure 4–32

6. Close the Find dialog box.

7. In the Navigation pane, in the *My Search Folders* area, select **All Assembly Models**. All results display in the Main table.

Task 5 - Delete the search for All Assembly Models.

In this task, you will delete a saved search.

1. Open the Find dialog box and select **File>Manage Saved Searches**.

2. In the Manage Saved Searches dialog box, select the **All Assembly Models** search.

3. Click **Delete**. In the Warning box, click **Yes** to confirm the deletion.

4. Click **OK** to complete the deletion and close the Manage Saved Searches dialog box.

5. Close the Find dialog box.

Task 6 - Create a saved search for Checked In Today using the Query Builder.

In this task, you will create a saved search using a date property using the Query Builder, and then save it to *My Search Folders*.

1. Click (Expand the query builder) next to the Quick Search.

2. Select Project Explorer ($) in the Navigation pane to search from the root folder. The Query Builder displays as shown in Figure 4–33.

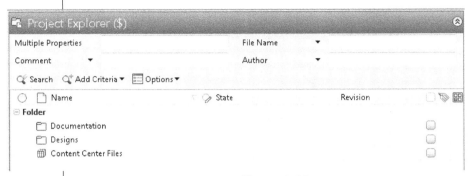

Figure 4–33

3. Click **Add Criteria** and select **Checked In**, as shown in Figure 4–34.

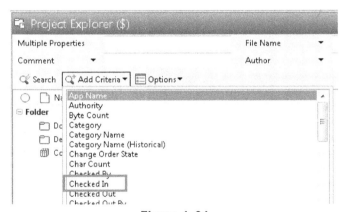

Figure 4–34

4. Expand the Checked In drop-down list as shown in Figure 4–35.

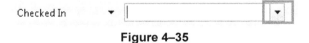

Figure 4–35

5. Select today's date from the calendar and click **Search**. The search results display.

6. Click **Options** and select **Save Search**, as shown in Figure 4–36.

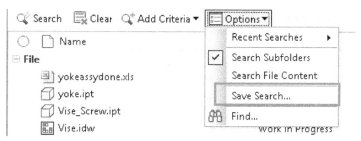

Figure 4–36

7. For the *Search Name*, enter **Checked In Today**.

8. Ensure that the **Save As Folder** option is selected, as shown in Figure 4–37.

Figure 4–37

9. Click **OK**.

10. In *My Search Folders*, select the **Checked In Today** search to view the results in the Main table.

Chapter Review Questions

1. How does the Basic Find search work?

   a. Enables you to navigate the folder structure to find and view design folders and files.

   b. The search locates the files and objects that match the specified file property criteria.

   c. The search locates any file or object in the vault that contains the search string in any of the file properties.

   d. All of the above.

2. What is not a valid search operator for a Basic or Advanced Find?

   a. *

   b. ?

   c. &

   d. NOT

3. What does the Advanced Find enable you to specify to refine your search? (Select all that apply.)

   a. Property Condition (e.g., is, <, >, etc.).

   b. Property Name

   c. Property Value

   d. Location in vault.

4. Where can saved searches be executed? (Select all that apply.)

   a. In the **Actions** menu.

   b. *My Search Folders* in the Navigation Pane.

   c. *My Shortcuts* in the Navigation Pane.

   d. In the Find dialog box, select **File>Open Search**.

5. Custom properties can be selected as search criteria.

   a. True

   b. False

Command Summary

Button	Command	Location
🔍 Find...	Find	• **Standard toolbar**
📂	**Open Search**	• **Find dialog box:** Toolbar
💾	**Save Current Search**	• **Find dialog box:** Toolbar

Chapter
5

Working with Non-CAD Files

When you get and check out files from the Autodesk® Vault software, the vault server downloads copies of the files from the vault to your working folder to make changes. Therefore, you are never directly making changes to the master copies. When viewing files, the server also downloads copies of the files to your working folder. These files are read-only until they are checked out. A file can only be checked out by one user at a time. After changes are made, the file is checked back into the vault.

Learning Objectives in this Chapter

- Differentiate between the functions and procedures of the Get, Check Out and Undo Check Out operations.
- Modify a checked out non-CAD file and then upload it to the vault using the Check In operation.
- Retrieve the latest version and previous version of a file.
- Differentiate between prompt and dialog box settings for streamlining the file check out and check in processes.
- Differentiate between the file status (vault status) icons, including the differences in their descriptions and required actions.

5.1 Get and Check Out

A file is checked out from the vault so that only one user can perform changes to the file. While the file is checked out, other users cannot modify the checked out files while they are in your control. They can only retrieve a read-only copy of the files until you perform a check in. Checking out temporarily increments the version of the file in the vault (e.g., a file at Version 1 becomes Version 2 on check out). After the changes to the file have been completed, you can check the file back into the vault server, where it remains at the incremented version (e.g. Version 2) and is available again for other users to check out and modify. Figure 5–1 shows a file that is crossed out, indicating that the file is checked out to another user, and a file that you currently have checked out.

Figure 5–1

One of three options can be used to check out a file: **Get, Check Out** or **Open**.

Get

The **Get** option is used to download a specified version of a file or files to a working folder. You can also choose to check out the file(s).

How To: Check Out a File Using the Get Option

1. Locate the files or use the search tools to locate the required files.
2. In the Main table or search results list, select the files to check out, right-click, and select **Get**. The Get dialog box opens as shown in Figure 5–2.

Use <Ctrl> to select multiple files.

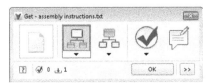

Figure 5–2

3. Click ⎡>>⎤ (Expand to show details). The expanded view of the Get dialog box displays, as shown in Figure 5–3.

By default, the Get dialog box is collapsed. If you want the dialog box to stay expanded every time you open it,

click ⤴ (Select the pin to lock the detail view).

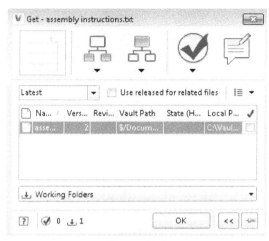

Figure 5–3

By default, the Get command downloads a read-only version of the file to the working folder without checking it out.

4. If you want to check out the file, click the checkbox in the Check Out column, as shown in Figure 5–4. You can also

click ✓ (Check Out Files) to automatically add the checkmark.

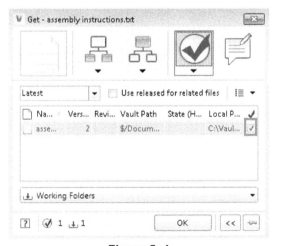

Figure 5–4

5. Click one or more of the buttons or options that are described as follows:

Option	Description
☑ Dependents / ☐ Attachments / ☑ Include Library Files	Click (Include Children) to automatically include specified children files when you check an object out of the vault. Click the drop-down arrow to select the children types that are included when the button is selected.
⊙ No Parents / ○ Direct Parents / ○ All Parents / ☑ Related Documentation	Click (Include Parents) to automatically include specified parent files when you check an object out of the vault. Click the drop-down arrow to select the parent types, if any, that are included when the button is clicked.
○ Source Selection / ⊙ All Files	Click (Check Out) to automatically select all of the objects listed for check out. Click the drop-down arrow to change your settings from *All Files* to **Source Selection** if you only want to select the files that were initially highlighted in the main view when you opened the Get/Check Out dialog box.
Working Folders / Working Folders / Working Folders - Force Overwrite / None / Browse...	Expand the *Working Folders* drop-down list to select the default working folder or browse to another folder in which to store the local copies of the objects that you download. You can also select **None** to not have a working folder.
Modify the second procedure	Click (Comments) to add a description or a comment stating why you are checking out the file, such as for a required modification.
Latest ▼	Set to **Latest** to copy the latest version of the file from the vault to the working folder. You can also select any past versions that are available in the vault.
☐ Use released for related files	Select this checkbox to get the released versions of all selected related files.

6. Review the files that are going to be checked out. The display can be controlled using the view icons, as shown in Figure 5–5.

Figure 5–5

7. Click 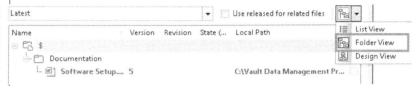 (Folder View) to display the selected files in a Folder view, as shown in Figure 5–6.

Figure 5–6

8. Click (List View) to display the files in a list as shown in Figure 5–7.

Figure 5–7

9. Click (Design View) to display the files to be checked out without their folder structure as shown in Figure 5–8.

Figure 5–8

10. If you want to exclude any of the displayed files from the selection that are going to be checked out, clear the check box next to their filenames.
11. Click **OK** to complete, which downloads the files to the working folder.

Check Out

You can use **Check Out** to perform a quick check out on a file. It bypasses the Get dialog box and always checks out the latest version of the file. Note that the file is checked out but not downloaded to the working folder.

How To: Check Out a File Using the Check Out Option

1. Locate the files or use the search tools to locate the required files.

Use <Ctrl> to select multiple files.

2. In the Main table or search results list, select the files to check out, right-click, and select **Check Out**. The files are immediately checked out but not downloaded, as shown in Figure 5–9.

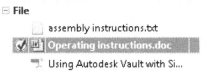

Figure 5–9

Open

You can use **Open** to check out the latest version of a file.

How To: Check Out a File using the Open Option

1. Locate the file or search for the required files using the search tools.

*You can also select **File>Open** or press <Ctrl>+<O>.*

2. In the Main table or search results list, select the file that you want to check out, right-click, and select **Open**. You are immediately prompted to check out the file, as shown in Figure 5–10.

Figure 5–10

3. Click **Yes** to check out the latest version of the file and open it in the associated application. It is also downloaded to the working folder.

5.2 Undo Check Out

If you have checked out a file but do not need to make changes to it, you can perform an **Undo Check Out** operation. This cancels the change operation to the selected file in the vault and your working folder, effectively setting the file back to the state it was before the check out operation. An **Undo Check Out** operation can also be performed on multiple files, or on a folder and all of its contents. Only the user who checked out the file can undo the check out.

How To: Undo a Check Out

1. Locate the files or search for the required files using the available search tools.
2. Select the files in the Main table or search results list, right-click, and select **Undo Check Out**. The Undo Check Out dialog box opens as shown in Figure 5–11.
   - You can also select **Actions>Undo Check Out** or click

     (Undo Check Out) in the Standard toolbar.

Multiple objects can be selected using <Ctrl>.

*To perform an **Undo Check Out** operation on an entire folder, select the folder, right-click, and select **Undo Check Out**.*

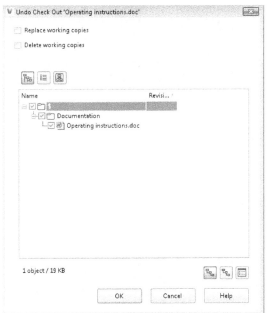

Figure 5–11

3. Select **Replace working copies** if you want the file in your working folder to return to the state it was in before you checked it out.

4. Select **Delete working copies** if you want the file in your working folder to be removed. This is a recommended best practice to ensure that you are always working with the latest version of the file.

5. Click (Settings) to control the inclusion settings of the children and parents of the selected files. The children are included by default.

6. Click **OK** to complete the operation.

5.3 Modifying Non-CAD Files

When a non-CAD file has been checked out, it can be modified and then checked in again. This enables you to use the version functionality on non-CAD files.

How To: Modify a Checked Out Non-CAD File

1. In the working folder select a file and open it in its associated application.
    - If the **Open** option was used, the application is opened automatically.
2. Make the required changes and save them. The changes are saved to your local working folder.
3. Check in the file.

5.4 Check In

After modifications are made to the file in the local working folder, the file can be checked back into the vault so that others can access the file with the latest changes.

How To: Check In a File

1. Locate the files or search for the required files using the search tools.

Multiple objects can be selected using <Ctrl>.

2. In the Main table or search results list, select the files to check in, right-click, and select **Check In**. The Check In dialog box opens as shown in Figure 5–12.

   • You can also select **Actions>Check In** or click

      (Check In) in the Standard toolbar.

Figure 5–12

3. Select **Keep files checked out** if you want to check the files back out immediately after checking them in.
4. Select **Delete working copies** to remove the local copy after the file is checked into the vault.
5. Click ▤ (Settings) to control the inclusion settings of the children and parents of the selected files. By default, the children are included.
6. In the *Enter comments to include...* area, enter any notes regarding this version.
7. Click **OK** to complete the operation.

5.5 File Versions

In the Get dialog box, you can download the latest version of the file to get or check out. You can also revert to a previous version, if required.

- Deleting the local copy of your files to ensure that you are always working with the latest version is a recommended best practice.

Latest Version

In the Get dialog box, use **Latest** to download the most current version of the selected files to your local working folder.

How To: Get the Latest Version of a File

1. Select the file, right-click, and select **Get**. The Get dialog box opens as shown in Figure 5–13.

   - You can also select **Actions>Get** or click ⬚ (Get) in the Standard toolbar.
   - Ensure that **Latest** is selected from the drop-down list.

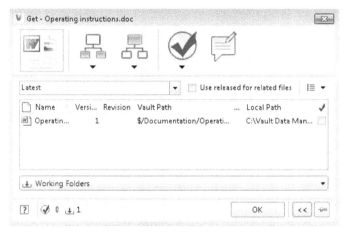

Figure 5–13

2. Click **Include Children** or **Include Parents** to control the inclusion settings of the children and parents of the selected file.
3. Click **OK** to complete the operation.

Previous Versions

There might be times when you want to revert back to a previous version of a file.

How To: Revert to a Previous Version of a File

1. Select a file, right-click on it, and select **Check Out**.
2. Select the *History* tab.
3. Select the **Show all versions** checkbox.
4. Select the file version that you would like to download, as shown in Figure 5–14.

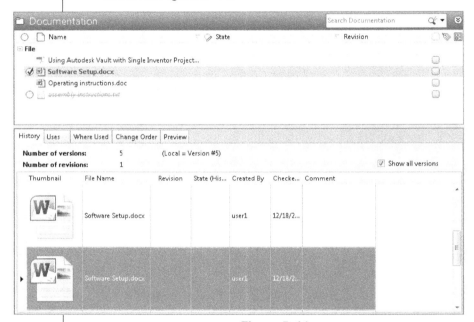

Figure 5–14

5. Right-click on the file and select **Get**.
6. Click **OK** to download to the working folder.
7. Click **Yes** when prompted to overwrite the working folder file with the file from the vault.
8. Now you can open the file from the working folder in the associated application and make any changes. Once it is checked back in to the Vault, it will be the latest version.

5.6 Managing Prompts and Dialog Boxes

To streamline the workflow process, you can manage the prompt and dialog box defaults that are related to lifecycle operations. In addition, you can specify which operations are performed automatically without prompting for input.

In the Autodesk Vault software, select **Tools>Options** to open the Options dialog box, as shown in Figure 5–15.

Figure 5–15

Prompts

To manage the default prompt settings, click **Prompts...** in the Options dialog box. The Manage Prompts dialog box opens as shown in Figure 5–16.

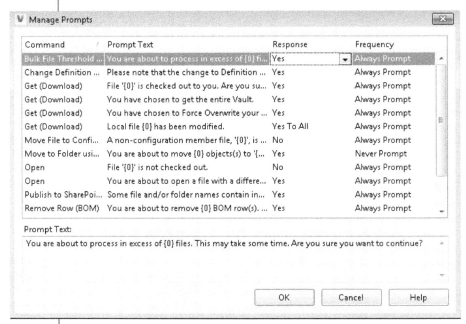

Figure 5–16

The dialog box displays four columns:

Command	Displays the command name.
Prompt Text	Displays the text that is displayed in the Warning box related to the selected command.
Response	Set the default response to the prompt.
Frequency	Set the frequency at which the prompt displays.

- Select **Always prompt** to open its dialog box each time. This is the default.
- Select **Never prompt** to use the answer that you select for the response as the new default.

Dialog Boxes

Dialog boxes associated with lifecycle operations can be customized and suppressed. If a dialog box is suppressed, it is not displayed when the operation is performed. This streamlines and automates the workflow process. In the *Dialog Suppression* area, select the dialog box option that you want to modify and click **Settings...** to open the related Settings dialog box.

The list of dialog boxes and their associated settings include those shown in Figure 5–17 and Figure 5–18:

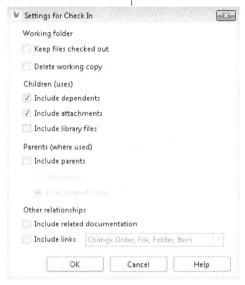

Settings for Check In dialog box

Figure 5–17

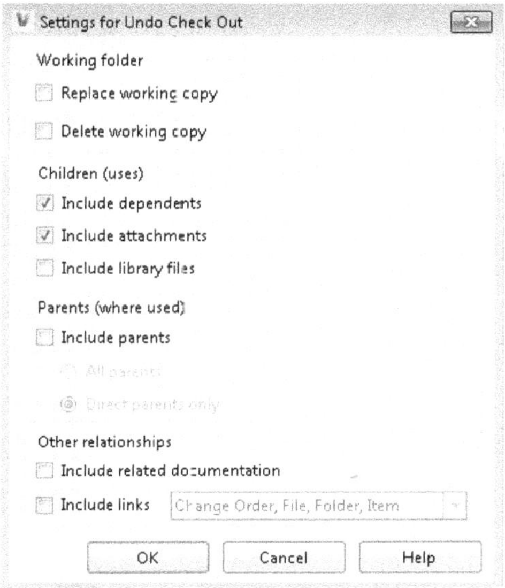

Settings for Undo Check Out dialog box

Figure 5–18

Document Preview

Use the *Document Preview* area to control document previews. Click **Document Previewers...** to open the Document Previewer Options dialog box, shown in Figure 5–19. Toggle a specific previewer by selecting the checkbox next to the option.

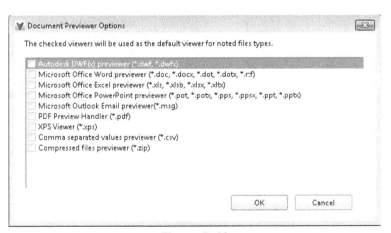

Figure 5–19

5.7 File Status

The status of a file in the vault, shown with vault status icons, status fonts, and modifiers, displays in the Autodesk Vault software and in the Autodesk Inventor Vault Browser.

- **Black/Normal font:** The file is not checked out

- **Blue/Bold:** The file is checked out to you. An asterisk beside the filename means that you have changes in memory that have not been saved

- **Gray/Italic/Strikethrough:** The file is checked out to another user.

- **Vault Status Modifier (+):** The file's edits have been saved locally.

Vault Status Icons

Icon	Description	Required Action
No icon	Indicates that the file is in the vault in a checked in state and that you do not have a local copy.	The file is available to be checked out, or a local copy can be retrieved using the **Get** command.
○ (empty)	The file is in the vault in a checked in state and the read-only version you are working on is the same as the one in the vault (also known as *Latest Version* or *leading version of the leading revision* of the file).	The read-only file is available to be checked out.
● (green)	The file is in the vault in a checked in state, but the version you are working on is newer than the latest version in the vault.	Typically means that your local file was changed without checking it out. To save any changes,
✔	The file is checked out to you and the version you are working on is the same as the one in the vault (also known as *Latest Version*).	Use **Check In** to check the file back into the vault or select **Undo Check Out** to cancel any changes.
△	The local copy is a historical revision of the leading revision in the vault.	=

(green)	The file is checked out to you but the version you are working on is newer than the latest version in the vault.	Typically means you made changes to the file since it was checked out but have not yet checked it back in.
	The file is not in the vault.	Use **Check In** to add the file to the vault.
	The local copy does not match the latest version in the vault.	Use the **Refresh from Vault** command to obtain the latest version of the file.
	The file is locked and the local copy is up-to-date.	
	The file is locked and the local copy is not up-to-date.	
	There has been an unexpected revision with the file, or the status could not be determined.	Review the tooltip for the action required.

Practice 5a | Modifying a Text File

Practice Objectives

- Locate and check out a text file.
- Modify a text file and check it back into the vault.
- Check out the file as another user.
- View the Vault Status and display the file's Version History.

In this practice, you will make modifications to an assembly instructions file. You will locate the file, check it out, make modifications, and then check it back into the vault. You will then check out the file as another user and as the original user, display the file's history.

Task 1 - Locate, Get, and Check Out a text file.

1. In the Autodesk Vault software, log in as **user1** without a password.

2. Locate the file **assembly instructions.txt**.

3. Select the file, right-click, and select **Get**.

4. In the Get dialog box, click $\boxed{>>}$ (Expand to show details) and ensure that it is set to **Latest**.

5. In the *Check Out* area, select the Check Out checkbox for

   assembly instructions.txt, or click ✅ (Check Out Files) to automatically select the file for check out. The dialog box updates as shown in Figure 5–20.

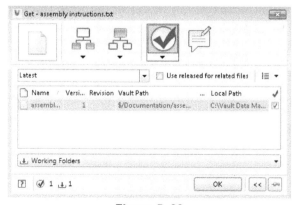

Figure 5–20

6. Click 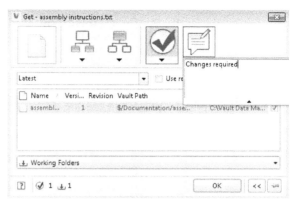 (Comments). In the text field, type **Changes required** as shown in Figure 5–21.

Figure 5–21

7. Click **OK**.

8. The Main table updates. Note that the vault status icon has updated to display and that the filename has a blue bold font. The file is checked out to you and the version you are working on is the same as the one in the vault (also known as the *Latest Version* or *leading version* of the leading revision of the file). The comments entered are also shown in the preview pane, as shown in Figure 5–22.

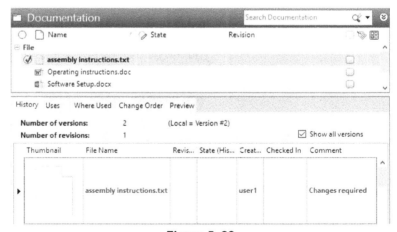

Figure 5–22

Task 2 - Open the text file and edit it.

In this task, you will open the text file in Notepad for modification.

1. Select **assembly instructions.txt**, right-click, and select **Open** to launch the Notepad application.

2. Edit the file in Notepad by adding the text: **4. Insert the 4 bolts into the holes.**

3. Save the file and exit Notepad.

4. In the Main table, refresh the display. The vault status icon updates to display a green circle with a checkmark ⊘, indicating that the file is checked out to you and that the version you are working on, in the working folder, is newer than the latest version in the vault. There is also a plus sign (+) in the Vault Status Modifier column, indicating the file's edits have been saved locally, as shown in Figure 5–23.

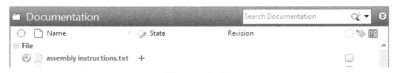

Figure 5–23

Task 3 - Check in the document.

In this task, you will release ownership of the file by checking it back into the vault. This is done to enable other users to view your modifications and add comments.

1. Select **assembly instructions.txt**, right-click, and select **Check In**.

2. Select **Delete working copies**. This is a recommended best practice.

3. In the *Enter comments to include...* area, type **Added step 4.** as shown in Figure 5–24. Click **OK**.

Figure 5–24

Task 4 - Check out the document as another user.

A co-worker now needs to add to the instructions.

1. Log out of the Autodesk Vault software by selecting **File>Log Out**.

2. Log back in as **user2** without a password.

3. Locate the **assembly instructions.txt** file, right-click and select **Get**.

4. Click ✅ (Check Out Files) to select the file for check out.

5. For the comment, type **Further modifications required** and click **OK** to perform the check out.

6. Log out of the Autodesk Vault software.

Task 5 - View vault status and display version history.

In this task, you will log back in as user1 and view the vault status and version history of the assembly instructions file.

1. Log in to the Autodesk Vault software as **user1**.

2. Locate the **assembly instructions.txt** file. Note that the file is crossed out, indicating that the file is checked out by someone else, as shown in Figure 5–25.

Figure 5–25

3. Select the file, right-click, and click **Get**. Click  (Expand to show details). Note that the **Check Out** option is not available in the Get dialog box because the file is checked out by **user2**, as shown in Figure 5–26.

Figure 5–26

4. Close the Get dialog box.

5. In the Preview pane, select the *History* tab to view the version history, as shown in Figure 5–27. Select **Show all versions** to show the version history.

Figure 5–27

Chapter Review Questions

1. When a file is checked out, no other users can modify it because it is set to a read-only status in the Autodesk Data Management Server.

   a. True

   b. False

2. What does an **Undo Check Out** operation do?

   a. Cancels the change operation to the selected file, increasing the version of the file.

   b. Cancels the change operation to the selected file, deleting the file from the database.

   c. Cancels the change operation to the selected file, keeping the file checked out.

   d. Cancels the change operation to the selected file, setting the file back to the state it was before the check out operation.

3. If Version 3 of a file is checked out, modified, checked back in, checked out again, and then an undo check out is performed, what is the version of the file in the database?

   a. 3

   b. 4

   c. 5

   d. 6

4. What are the steps for reverting to a previous version of a file?

a. Use **Check Out**, and then open the file from the working folder.

b. Check Out the file. In the file's *History* tab, ensure that the **Show all versions** option is selected, and then select the required version. Right-click, select **Get**, and then click **OK** to download.

c. Use **Get**, select the previous version from the list, then use the **Open from Vault** command to open the previous version from the vault database.

d. Use **Get**, select the previous version from the list, then open the file from the working folder.

e. Use **Get**, select the latest version from the list, then open the file from the working folder.

5. What is the file status of an icon showing a white circle with a checkmark ( )?

a. The file is checked out to you and the version you are working on is the same as the one in the vault.

b. The file is checked out to you but there is no local copy in the working folder.

c. The file is checked out by another user and the read-only version you are working on is the same as the one in the vault.

d. The file is checked out to you but the version you are working on is newer than the latest version in the vault.

Command Summary

Button	Command	Location
	Check In	• **Menu:** Actions>Check In • **Shortcut:** (*right-click on selected file*) • **Standard Toolbar**
	Get	• **Menu:** Actions>Get • **Shortcut:** (*right-click on selected file*) • **Standard Toolbar**
	Check Out	• **Menu:** Actions>Check Out • **Shortcut:** (*right-click on selected file*)
	Undo Check Out	• **Menu:** Actions>Undo Check Out • **Shortcut:** (*right-click on selected file*) • **Standard Toolbar**

Working with Autodesk Inventor CAD Files

As with non-CAD files, the Autodesk® Vault software records the process of change in an Autodesk Inventor file when you use the Autodesk Vault software and Vault Add-in to check out files from the vault. In this chapter you learn how to change the lifecycle states and revisions for Autodesk Inventor designs.

Learning Objectives in this Chapter

- Check out Autodesk® Inventor® files in the Autodesk Inventor software using multiple methods.
- Undo a Check Out operation using Undo Check Out in the Autodesk Inventor software.
- Modify checked out Autodesk Inventor files and use Check In to upload files back to the vault.
- Download the previous version of a file.
- Change the lifecycle states and create new revisions of Autodesk Inventor files.
- Differentiate between prompt and dialog box settings for streamlining the Autodesk Inventor file check out and check in processes.

6.1 Check Out Autodesk Inventor Files

A file is checked out from the vault so that only one person can perform changes to the file. While the file is checked out, other users cannot modify the checked out files while they are in your control. They can only retrieve a read-only copy of the files until you perform a check in. For Autodesk Inventor files, you can select one of the following four methods to check out the latest version of a file:

- In the Autodesk Inventor software with a read-only file opened from the vault, select the components to be checked out, right-click and select **Vault>Check Out**.

- Check out a file using **Open** in the *Vault* tab>Access panel in the Autodesk Inventor software. You will be prompted to check out.

- Check out from the Vault Browser.

- Check out a file using the **Open** option in the Autodesk Vault software. You will be prompted to check out.

Check Out by Selecting Components

A read-only file that has been opened from the Vault should be explicitly checked out if you are to make changes to it. You can check out the file at any time in the Model Browser.

How To: Check Out a File in the Autodesk Inventor Software

1. In the Model browser, right-click the component to be checked out and select **Vault>Check Out**.
2. The standard Check Out dialog box opens. Select **Get latest version**, as shown in Figure 6–1 to ensure that the latest version is checked out. If this option is not selected, the currently open, read-only version of the file is checked out. You cannot specifically select which version is being checked out.

Figure 6–1

Check Out using Open From Vault

You can use **Open** in the *Vault* tab>Access panel to check out the latest file from the vault when you open it in the Autodesk Inventor software. This is a different function from the standard Autodesk Inventor **Open** command where the file is opened directly from the vault.

How To: Check Out a File in the Autodesk Inventor Software

1. In the *Vault* tab>Access panel, click 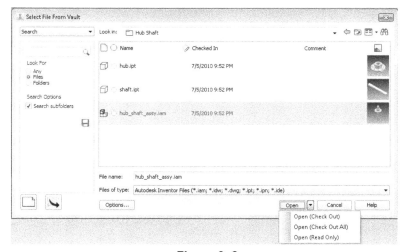 (Open).
2. In the Select File From Vault dialog box, expand **Open**, and select one of the check out options: **Open (Check Out)**, **Open (Check Out All)**, or **Open (Read Only)** as shown in Figure 6–2.

Figure 6–2

If you click **Open** when retrieving an Autodesk Inventor file and the file is available for check out, a Warning box opens prompting you to check the file out, as shown in Figure 6–3.

Figure 6–3

Check Out From the Vault Browser

If you decide to open the file as read-only from the vault, you can check out the file at any time through the Vault Browser.

How To: Check Out a File from the Vault Browser

1. In the Vault Browser, right-click on the file and select **Check Out**, as shown in Figure 6–4.

Figure 6–4

2. The Check Out dialog box opens. Select **Get latest version**, as shown in Figure 6–5 to ensure that the latest version is checked out. If this option is not selected, the currently open, read-only version of the file is checked out. You cannot specifically select which version is being checked out.

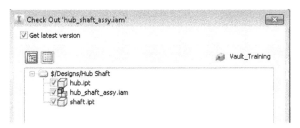

Figure 6–5

3. Click **Settings...** to control the inclusion settings of the children and parents of the selected files.
4. In the *Enter comments to include...* area, type comments to explain the changes to this version.
5. Click **OK** to complete the operation.

Check Out using Open in Autodesk Vault

In the Autodesk Vault software, you can check out the file at any time using the **Open** option when prompted. Using this option you cannot specify which version of the file is being checked out. The latest version is automatically checked out.

How To: Check Out an Autodesk Inventor File Using the Open Option

1. Locate the file or search for the required files using the search tools.
2. In the Main table or search results area, select the file that you want to check out, right-click, and select **Open**, as shown in Figure 6–6.

Figure 6–6

3. In the Open File dialog box, select **Yes** to open and check out the file, or **No** to open without checking out the file, as shown in Figure 6–7.

Figure 6–7

6.2 Undo Check Out in Autodesk Inventor

If you have checked out a file but do not need to make changes to it, you can perform an **Undo Check Out** operation. This cancels the change operation to the selected file in the vault and your working folder, effectively setting the file back to the state it was in before the check out operation. An **Undo Check Out** operation can also be performed on multiple files, or on a folder and all of its contents. Only the user who checked out the file can undo the check out.

How To: Undo a Check Out

1. In the Autodesk Inventor software, in the Vault Browser, select the file, right-click, and select **Undo Check Out**. The Undo Check Out dialog box opens, as shown in Figure 6–8.

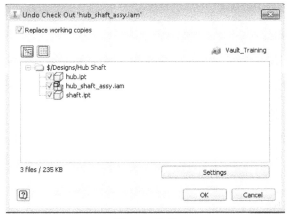

Figure 6–8

2. Select **Replace working copies** if you want to replace the local file with the version that is currently stored in the vault.
3. Click **Settings...** to control the settings of the children and parents of the selected files and the visualization options (whether .DWF files are created). The children are included by default.
4. Click **OK**.

6.3 Modifying Autodesk Inventor Files

The vault enables multiple users to access the same design project and work on different parts of the design.

For example, user1 can be working on part A of an assembly and user2 on part B of the same assembly. They can both retrieve a read-only copy of the assembly to their working folders and only check out the part for modification. If you try to modify a file that has not yet been checked out, a message box opens prompting you to do so, as shown in Figure 6–9.

*To change the settings for the **File Edit** prompt, in the Vault tab>File Status panel, select **Vault Options**, click **Prompts...** and change the response or frequency for **File Edit**.*

Figure 6–9

After modifications are performed, a file must be saved in Autodesk Inventor before a **Check In** operation can be performed. By default, if you try to close a checked out Autodesk Inventor file without checking it in, the system prompts you to save the file and check it in.

6.4 Check In Autodesk Inventor Files

After modifications are made to the file in the local working folder and it is saved, the file can be checked back into the vault so that other users can access the file containing the latest changes.

How To: Check In an Autodesk Inventor File

1. In the Vault Browser, select the file, right-click, and select **Check In**. The Check In dialog box opens as shown in Figure 6–10.

For manual check in operations, you can scan and include local documentation related to the 3D model or not by toggling between

(Related files are excluded for the check-in operation) and

(Related files are included for the check-in operation).

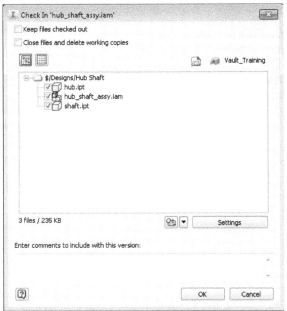

Figure 6–10

2. Select **Keep files checked out** if you want to keep the files checked out for further modifications.
3. Select **Close files and delete working copies** to remove the local copy after the file is checked into the vault. This is a recommended best practice. If required, close the file in the Autodesk Inventor software.

4. Click **Settings** to control the inclusion settings of the children and parents of the selected files. You can also specify whether or not .DWF files are automatically created and attached to the files by setting the Visualization Attachment options, as shown in Figure 6–11.

Figure 6–11

5. In the *Enter comments to include...* area, type comments to explain the changes for this version.
6. Click **OK** to complete the operation.

6.5 Get Previous Versions

To retrieve older versions of Autodesk Inventor part files from Autodesk Vault, you must be in the Autodesk Vault software and use the **Get** command. It cannot be done directly in the Autodesk Inventor software.

Note: If you need to restore previous versions of complete assemblies, Labels can be used. Details on how to create Labels are covered in another chapter.

How To: To Revert to a Previous Version

1. Select the file, right-click on it, and then select **Check Out**.
2. Select the *History* tab.
3. Select **Show all versions**.
4. Select the version of the file that you would like to download.
5. Right-click on the file and click **Get**.
6. The previous version of the file is shown in the dialog box. Click **OK** to download to the working folder.
7. Click **Yes** when prompted to overwrite the working folder file with the file from the vault.
8. Now you can open the file from the working folder in Autodesk Inventor and make any changes. Once it is checked back in to the vault, it will be the latest version.

6.6 Changing Lifecycle States and Next Release/Revision Procedures

Change State

The **Change State** command enables you to change the lifecycle state of a selected object.

How To: Change State

1. Select the objects from the main pane.
2. Click **Change State**, or right-click and select **Change State**.
3. Select a lifecycle definition, if required, and then select the lifecycle state from the drop-down list.
4. Click **Settings** for children and parent options, if required.
5. Enter a comment or predefined comment.
6. Click **OK**.

The following is a list of predefined Lifecycle States for the Flexible Release Process that is associated with the Engineering Category:

State Name	Description
Work In Progress	Also known as WIP, this state typically involves the editing of the files. By default, the Revision will increment when the state is changed to WIP.
For Review/In Review	In general, no editing is permitted at this state.
Released	Typically read-only access where editing is not permitted.
Obsolete	Designs are no longer active and therefore access is restricted. Typically, no edits can be made.

Change Revision / Revise

The **Change Revision** and **Revise** commands create a new revision of a file or item.

The **Revise** command is found in Autodesk Inventor in the *Vault* tab. The **Change Revision** command is found in Autodesk Vault in the **Actions** menu or toolbar.

When you need to make changes to a file or item that has already been released into production, you must first create a new revision. This protects the integrity of the existing released version, and creates a new version on which to make the changes. When a file is revised, its revision is incremented following a predefined sequence, and the version number is reset to 1.

How To: Create a New Revision in Autodesk Inventor

1. In Autodesk Inventor, open the file you want to revise.
2. In the *Vault* tab, click **Revise**, as shown in Figure 6–12.

Figure 6–12

3. Select one of the format options shown in Figure 6–13.

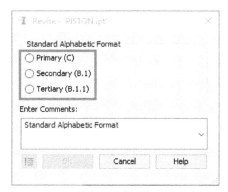

Figure 6–13

4. Click **OK**.

How To: Create a New Revision in Autodesk Vault

1. In Autodesk Vault, select a file and then in the toolbar, select **Change Revision**.
2. In the Select next revision drop-down list, select **Primary**, **Secondary**, or **Tertiary**, as shown in Figure 6–14.

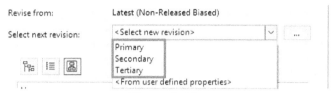

Figure 6–14

3. Click **OK**.

Released Biased

Released Biased is an option that determines if released objects should take priority over unreleased objects. This option can be toggled on and off as shown in Figure 6–15. The **Released Biased** toggle is also available when opening or placing Inventor files.

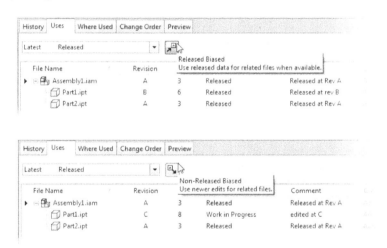

Figure 6–15

6.7 Get Revision

You can retrieve a specific revision of a file, if and when required.

How To: Get a Specific Revision

1. In the Autodesk Inventor software, select **Get Revision**, as shown in Figure 6–16.

Figure 6–16

The Revision drop-down list is also available when opening or placing Autodesk Inventor files in the vault.

2. Select a revision from the Select Revision drop-down list, as shown in Figure 6–17.

Figure 6–17

3. Click **OK**.

Roll Back Lifecycle State Change

Another method to revert to a previous revision is to undo the revision change using the **Roll Back Lifecycle State Change** command.

How To: Roll Back a File's Lifecycle State

1. Select a file in the main table and select **Actions>Roll Back Lifecycle State Change...**, as shown in Figure 6–18.

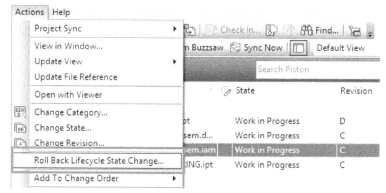

Figure 6–18

2. A window opens describing to which state the file will be rolled back. Click **Yes** to continue and complete the lifecycle state rollback, as shown in Figure 6–19.

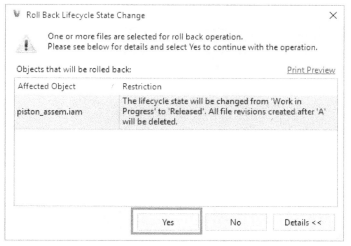

Figure 6–19

6.8 Vault Revision Tables

The Vault Revision Table feature enables you to automatically update a drawing's revision table with Vault data when its properties are synchronized through the Job Server. You can also synchronize the properties manually.

How To: Add a Vault Revision Table to a Drawing

1. In the *Annotate* tab, click **Vault Revision**, as shown in Figure 6–20.

Figure 6–20

2. Insert the table in the drawing, as shown in Figure 6–21.

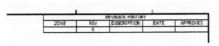

Figure 6–21

3. To edit the table, right-click on the revision table and select **Edit**. as shown in Figure 6–22.

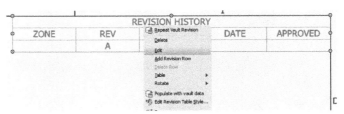

Figure 6–22

4. To remove a column, right-click on a column header and click **Column Chooser...** as shown in Figure 6–23.

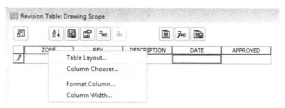

Figure 6–23

5. Select the column to be removed in the *Selected Properties* list and click **Remove**, as shown in Figure 6–24.

Figure 6–24

6. Click **OK**. The revision table updates with the change, as shown in Figure 6–25.

REVISION HISTORY			
REV	DESCRIPTION	DATE	APPROVED
A			

Figure 6–25

Update Properties

The Update Properties feature is integrated with the vault revision table, ensuring that revision block data is synchronized with vault release information. You can manually update the properties if mapped properties are edited in several ways, as shown in Figure 6–26 by using Update Properties in the Vault Browser or Vault tab, or by right-clicking on the Vault Revision table and select **Populate with vault data**.

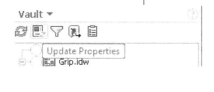

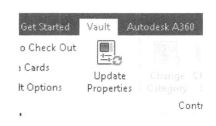

Figure 6–26

6.9 PDF Creation

You can automatically publish 2D PDF files from your Autodesk Inventor files when releasing your designs.

By default, PDF files created from 2D Inventor files are attached to the 2D design file being released and can be viewed in the *Uses* tab, as shown in Figure 6–27.

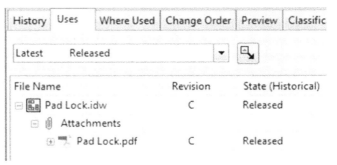

Figure 6–27

6.10 Managing Prompts and Dialog Boxes

To streamline the workflow process, you can customize the prompt and dialog box defaults that are related to **Check In**, **Check Out** and **Undo Check Out** operations. In addition, you can specify which operations are performed automatically without prompting for your input.

In Autodesk Inventor, in the *Vault* tab>File Status panel, click

 (Vault Options) to open the Options dialog box, as shown in Figure 6–28.

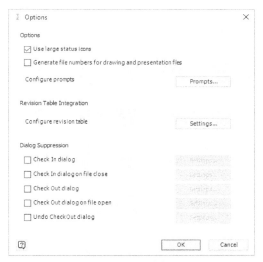

Figure 6–28

Prompts

To manage the default prompt settings, click **Prompts...** in the *Options* area. The Manage Prompts dialog box opens as shown in Figure 6–29.

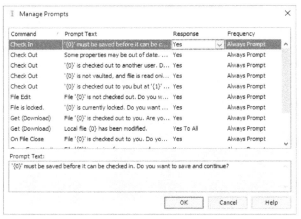

Figure 6–29

The dialog box displays four columns:

Command	Displays the command name.
Prompt Text	Displays the text that is displayed in the Warning box related to the selected command.
Response	Set the default response to the prompt.
Frequency	Set the frequency at which the prompt displays. • Select **Always prompt** to open the prompt dialog box each time. This is the default. • Select **Never prompt** to use the answer that you select for the response as the new default.

Dialog Boxes

Dialog boxes associated with Check In, Check Out, Undo Check Out, and file open and close operations can be customized with default settings and suppressed. When the operation is performed, no dialog box opens, therefore streamlining and automating the workflow. In the *Dialog Suppression* area, select the dialog box option that you want to modify and click **Settings...** to open the related Settings dialog box.

The list of dialog boxes and their associated settings are shown in Figure 6–30 to Figure 6–34:

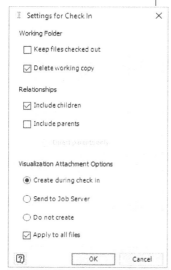

Settings for Check In dialog box

Figure 6–30

Settings for Check In dialog box on file close

Figure 6–31

Settings for Check Out dialog box

Figure 6–32

Settings for Check Out dialog box on file open

Figure 6–33

Settings for Undo Check Out dialog box

Figure 6–34

Practice 6a

Modifying an Autodesk Inventor Design

Practice Objectives

- Locate and check out an Autodesk Inventor assembly.
- Modify a part in an Autodesk Inventor assembly, check the assembly back into the vault and display the version history.
- Use the Vault Browser to view vault status and display the Autodesk Inventor design's version history.

In this practice, you will check out an Autodesk Inventor assembly, make changes, and then check it back into the vault.

Task 1 - Open an assembly from the vault.

In this task, you will open and check out an assembly from the Autodesk Vault software using the **Open** option.

1. In the Autodesk Vault software, select the *$\Designs\Mold Assembly* folder. Select **Final Mold Assy.iam**, right-click, and select **Open** to launch the Autodesk Inventor software. In the Warning box, click **Yes** to check out the assembly. The Autodesk Inventor software is launched (if this is not already done) and the assembly is opened.

Task 2 - Modify a part.

In this task, you will make a modification to the height of the Grip Handle part. Since only the assembly was originally checked out, you will be prompted to check out the Grip Handle part when making the modification.

1. In the Model Browser, right-click on **Grip handle:1** and select **Edit**.

2. Select **Extrusion1**, right-click, and select **Show Dimensions**.

3. Modify the height of the Grip Handle from *1.5 inches* to **6** *inches*.

4. In the Warning box, click **Yes** to check out **Grip handle.ipt**.

5. Update the model in the Autodesk Inventor software and return to the assembly. The assembly updates as shown in Figure 6–35.

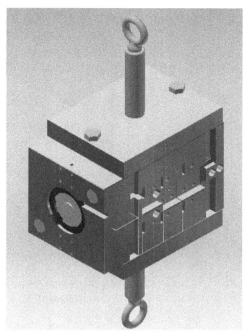

Figure 6–35

Task 3 - View the Vault Browser icons.

In this task, you will view the Vault Browser to see how it changes after the part has been modified.

1. Open the Vault Browser to display the files, as shown in Figure 6–36. The Grip Handle part displays in blue with an asterisk, indicating that it has been changed and requires a save.

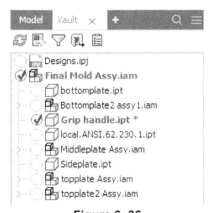

Figure 6–36

In the Vault Browser, the vault status icon for the checked out files is a circle with a checkmark (✔). It indicates that you are working on the latest version of the files and that they are checked out to you.

2. In the Quick Access Toolbar, select 🖫 (Save).

3. Click **OK** to save **Final Mold Assy.iam** and all of its dependents. The vault status icon for the saved Grip handle part turns green. This indicates that the file you are working on is newer than the one in the vault.

Task 4 - Check In the files.

In this task, you will check the modified files into the vault to make them accessible to other users.

1. In the Vault Browser, right-click on **Final Mold Assy.iam** and select **Check In**.

2. In the Check In dialog box, in the *Enter comments to include...*area, type **Modified the grip handle**.

3. Click **Settings** to view whether or not children and parents are included when checking in and if .DWF attachments are to be created. By default, **Include children**, **Create visualization attachment**, and **Apply to all files** are selected. Leave the settings as they are and click **OK**.

4. In the Check In dialog box, click **OK** to complete the check in.

5. In the Warning box, click **Yes** to the confirm the deletion of files in the local working folder.

Task 5 - Display the design history.

In this task, you will open **Final Mold Assy.iam** again and view its design history.

1. In the Autodesk Inventor software, in the *Vault* tab>Access panel, click 🗐 (Open).

2. In the *$\Designs\Mold Assembly* folder, double-click on **Final Mold Assy.iam** to open the assembly as read-only (default).

3. In the Warning box click **No**.

4. Open the Vault Browser.

5. Right-click on **Final Mold Assy.iam** and select **Show Details**. The Details window opens, displaying the version history with images of **Final Mold Assy.iam**. Select **Show all versions**.

Note the Grip Handle change, as shown in Figure 6–37.

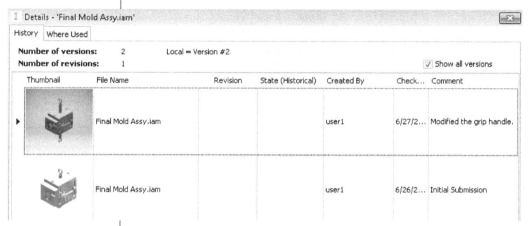

Figure 6–37

6. Close the Details window.

7. Close **Final Mold Assy.iam**.

Task 6 - Display the version numbers in Autodesk Vault.

In this task, you will view the part version numbers in the Autodesk Vault software that are associated with **Final Mold Assy.iam**.

1. In the Autodesk Vault software, click ⟳ (Refresh). Only **Final Mold Assy.iam** and **Grip handle.ipt** have 2 versions. All other parts in the design remain at one version. The status icon also indicates that all of the files are checked in.

Practice 6b

Get a Previous Version of an Inventor Part

Practice Objectives

- Use the Get command to download a previous version of an Autodesk Inventor part file to your working folder.
- Make changes to the part, save it, check it back in to the vault and view its version history.
- Modify the dialog box default when closing the file.

In this practice, you will use **Get** to roll back an Inventor part file to a previous version, because changes in the latest version are no longer required. You will also manage the dialog box defaults used on **File Close**.

Task 1 - Get the previous version of a file.

In this task, you will use the **Get** command to download a previous version of the shaft part to your local working folder.

1. In the Autodesk Vault software, in the Navigation pane, select the *$\Designs\Hub Shaft* folder to display its design files.

2. In the Main table, right-click on **shaft.ipt** and select **Check Out**.

3. In the Preview pane for **shaft.ipt**, select the *History* tab. Select **Show all versions**, if required. You need to go back to the original version, Version 1, with the original, shorter shaft length.

4. Select **Version 1**, and then right-click on **shaft.ipt** and select **Get**. Note that the image shows the shorter length of shaft. Click **OK** to download the file to the working folder.

5. If prompted, select **Yes** to overwrite the file in the working folder with the file from the vault. The Vault status icon

   updates to show ⟳ with the tooltip showing incorrect version, which is the desired effect in this case. In other words, the local copy does not match the latest version in the vault.

6. Now you can open the file from the working folder in Autodesk Inventor and make any changes, as shown in the next tasks. Once it is checked back in to the vault, it will be the latest version.

Task 2 - Open a previous version in Autodesk Inventor.

In this task, you will open Version 1 of the Shaft part into the Autodesk Inventor software from the local working folder.

1. In the Autodesk Inventor software, in the *Get Started* tab> Launch panel, click 🗁 (Open). You are not selecting **Open** in the *Vault* tab because you need to retrieve the local copy of the file.

2. In the *Hub Shaft* folder, select **shaft.ipt** and open it. This is the version with the shorter shaft.

Task 3 - Make changes and save the shaft part.

In this task, you will make modifications to make that version the latest.

1. Open the Vault Browser. In the Autodesk Inventor software, the vault status icon also shows the red arrows 🔄, indicating the version you are working with is older than the latest version in the vault.

2. Open the Model Browser, right-click **Extrusion**, and select **Show Dimensions**. Modify the diameter from 35 to **30 mm**.

3. Open the Vault Browser. **shaft.ipt** displays blue bold font with an asterisk, indicating that a save is required. as shown in Figure 6–38.

Figure 6–38

4. In the Quick Access Toolbar, click 💾 (Save).

5. In the Data Format Has Changed dialog box, click **OK**. The Data Format has changed because Version 1 was created in a previous Autodesk Inventor version and you are now saving it in the latest Autodesk Inventor version. The vault status icon changes, indicating that a check in is required.

Task 4 - Check in modified part.

In this task, you will check in the modified part.

1. Select **shaft.ipt**, right-click, and select **Check In**.

2. In the Check In dialog box, in the *Enter comments to include...* area, type **Changed diameter of shaft**. Clear the **Close files and delete working copies** option.

3. Click **OK**. The file was not closed because **Close files and delete working copies** was not selected when checking in. The vault status icons indicate that you are now working on the latest version.

4. Select **shaft.ipt,** right-click on it, and select **Show Details**. Select **Show all versions**. The results are shown in Figure 6–39.

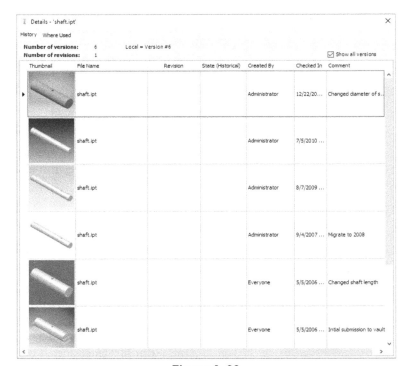

Figure 6–39

5. Close the Details window.

6. Close the **shaft.ipt**.

Task 5 - Modify the dialog box default when closing the file.

In this task, you will modify the default settings when closing an Autodesk Inventor file so that working copies are deleted by default.

1. In the Autodesk Inventor software, in the *Vault* tab, expand the Access panel, and click 🗀 (Go to Workspace). Browse to the *Hub Shaft* folder to verify that the design files are present. Close Windows Explorer.

2. In the *Vault* tab>File Status panel, click ▦ (Vault Options).

3. Select **Check In dialog on file close** and click **Settings** next to **Check in dialog on file close**.

4. Select **Delete working copy** and click **OK** to set that option as the new default.

5. In the Options dialog box, click **OK**.

6. Exit Autodesk Inventor.

Task 6 - Open and close the assembly file.

In this task, you will see the effect of setting the **Delete working copy** option as the default when closing an Autodesk Inventor file.

1. In the Autodesk Vault software, click 🔄 (Refresh).

2. In the $\Designs\Hub Shaft folder, select **hub_shaft_assy.iam**, right-click, and select **Open**. Check out and open the assembly in the Autodesk Inventor software.

3. Close the assembly file. Save and **Check In**.

4. In the *Vault* tab, expand the Access panel, and click 🗀 (Go to Workspace). Browse to the $\Designs\Hub Shaft folder to verify that the files have now been deleted. Only .DWF files are in the folder.

5. Close the Workspace window.

Practice 6c | Revising an Inventor Design

Practice Objectives

- Change the lifecycle state and revisions of files.
- Change the revision of a file.
- Retrieve a previous revision of a design.

In this practice, you will revise design files using the **Change State** and the **Change Revision** commands.

Task 1 - Release Piston Design Assembly.

1. In the Autodesk Vault software, navigate to the
   $\Designs\Piston$ folder. Note that all files are at Revision **A**
   and that the States are all **Work in Progress**.

2. Select **piston_assem.iam**, right-click on it, and then select
   Change State.

3. Select **Released** from the drop-down list, and then click
   Include Dependents. The comments automatically display
   Released to manufacturing, as shown in Figure 6–40.

Figure 6–40

4. Click **OK**. The results display as shown in Figure 6–41. Note
   that all of the design files are still at *Revision* **A**, and that
   State is now set to **Released** with the files locked.

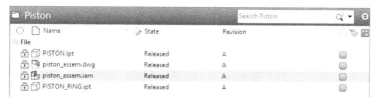

Figure 6–41

Task 2 - Create a New Revision using Change State.

1. In Autodesk Vault, select **PISTON.ipt**, right-click on it, and then select **Change State**.

2. Select **Work In Progress**, as shown in Figure 6–42.

Figure 6–42

3. Click **OK**. The *Revision* changes to **B** as shown Figure 6–43.

Figure 6–43

4. Open **PISTON.ipt** in Autodesk Inventor and click **Yes** to check out the file. Typically you would now make a design change and check in the file again. In the Vault Browser, right-click on **PISTON.ipt** and select **Check In**. Then click **OK**.

5. View the results in Autodesk Vault. Note that the file is still at *Revision* **B**.

Task 3 - Create a New Revision using Change Revision.

1. In Autodesk Vault, select **PISTON.ipt** and then in the toolbar select **Change Revision**.

2. Select **Secondary**. The revision for the file changes to **B.1**.

3. Enter **design variation** in the *Enter comments* field. Click **OK**.

Task 4 - View the Uses tab of assembly in Autodesk Vault.

1. In Autodesk Vault, select **piston_assem.iam** and select the *Uses* tab. The default display shows the Non-Released Biased configuration. The Piston Assembly shows the Work In Progress B.1 Version of the **PISTON.ipt** as a child, as shown in Figure 6–44.

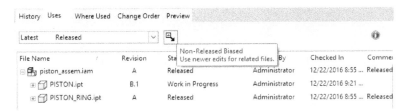

Figure 6–44

2. Select **Non-Released Biased** in the *Uses* tab to change it to **Released Biased**. Review the results. Note that when you use the **Released Biased** option, the Piston Assembly displays the Released A Version of the PISTON as a child, as shown in Figure 6–45.

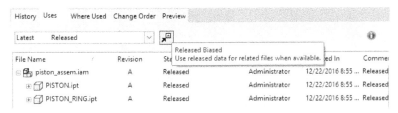

Figure 6–45

3. Change the state of PISTON to **Released** and note the change when set to Released Biased.

Practice 6d | Creating a Vault Revision Table

Practice Objective

- Add a Vault Revision Table to an Inventor drawing.

In this practice, you will add a Vault revision table to a drawing.

Task 1 - Add a Revision Table to drawing.

1. In Autodesk Vault, select **piston_assem.dwg**, right-click on it, and then select **Change State**. Select **Work in Progress**.

2. In Autodesk Vault, select **piston_assem.dwg**, right-click on it, and open it in Autodesk Inventor. Click **Yes** to check it out.

3. In the *Annotate* tab, click **Vault Revision**, as shown in Figure 6–46.

Figure 6–46

4. Insert the table in the top right corner of the drawing.

5. Right-click on the revision table and select **Edit**. Remove the *Zone* column.

6. Save the drawing and check it into the vault using the **Close files and delete the working copies** option.

7. Now you can use the **Change State** command to release the files and then view the changes to the Vault Revision Table.

8. Click **Update Properties** in the Vault Browser to manually update the table. Alternatively, the Vault administrator can set the environment to update the properties automatically when revisions are made to files in the Vault.

Chapter Review Questions

1. A file needs to be checked out to modify it.

   a. True

   b. False

2. While working on a checked out file in the Autodesk Inventor software, how can you retrieve the latest version of the file thereby discarding any changes made?

   a. In the Vault Browser, right-click the file and select **Refresh File**.

   b. In the Vault Browser, right-click the file and select **Show Details**.

   c. In the *Vault* tab>Access panel, select **Open**. In the Select File From Vault dialog box, click **Open**.

   d. In the Vault Browser, right-click on the file and select **Undo Check Out**.

3. In Figure 6–47, what does the highlighted button indicate?

   a. Related files are included for the check-in operation.

   b. Related files are excluded for the check-in operation.

Figure 6–47

4. By default, .DWF files are automatically created and attached to the files on check in.

   a. True

   b. False

5. What does the red arrows ( ) vault status icon indicate?

   a. The file is locked and the local copy is up-to-date

   b. The local copy is a historical revision of the leading revision in the vault.

   c. The file is not in the vault. Use Check In to add the file to the vault.

   d. The local copy does not match the latest version in the vault. Use the Refresh from Vault command to obtain the latest version of the file.

Command Summary

Button	Command	Location
	Check In	• **Inventor Ribbon:** *Vault* tab>File Status panel • Shortcut menu in the Vault Browser
	Get	• **Menu:** Actions>Get • **Shortcut:** (*right-click on selected file*) • **Standard Toolbar**
	Check Out	• **Menu:** Actions>Check Out • **Shortcut:** (*right-click on selected file*)
	Refresh File	• **Inventor Ribbon:** *Vault* tab>File Status panel • Shortcut menu in the Vault Browser
	Undo Check Out	• **Inventor Ribbon:** *Vault* tab>File Status panel • Shortcut menu in the Vault Browser

Customizing the User Interface

You can customize the user interface of the Autodesk® Vault software to improve productivity and efficiency.

Learning Objectives in this Chapter

- Customize the Autodesk Vault interface using the View menu.
- Change the column display in the Autodesk Vault software using the Customize View option.
- Apply a filter to the main table using the filter options.
- Create a custom view using the Define custom views menu.
- Create a shortcut to access frequently used designs.

7.1 Autodesk Vault Customization

The **View** menu options control the display of the Autodesk Vault window. The menu is shown in Figure 7–1.

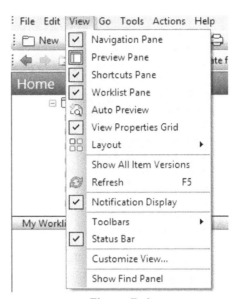

Figure 7–1

Pane Display

You can toggle the interface items shown in Figure 7–2 on and off.

Standard Toolbar

Advanced Toolbar

Navigation Pane

Shortcuts Pane

Preview Pane

Find Panel

Status Bar

Properties Grid

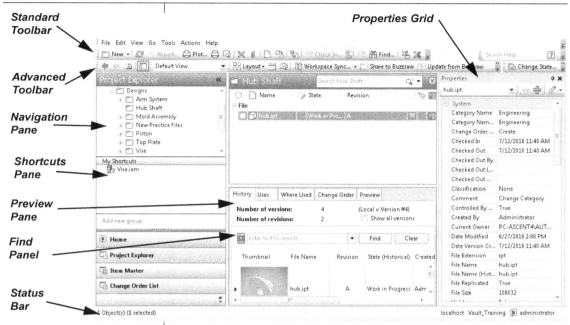

Figure 7–2

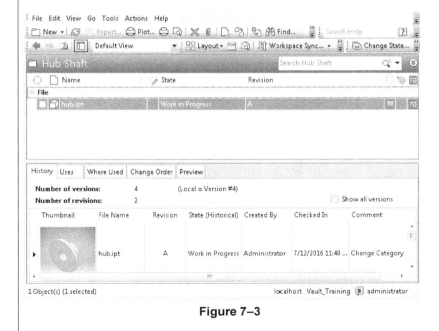 *(Preview pane) is also located in the Advanced toolbar.*

If a window pane is on (displayed), you can toggle it off (hide it) by selecting its option in the **View** menu. For example, you can toggle the Navigation pane and the Properties grid off so that the Main table and Preview pane fill the extra space, as shown in Figure 7–3.

Figure 7–3

Auto Preview

Auto Preview can also be toggled on or off in either the View menu or from the Advanced toolbar (). When on, objects display in the Main table with comments directly below them, as shown in Figure 7–4.

Figure 7–4

7.2 Customizing Columns

The **Customize View** option enables you to customize the column display in the Main table, Preview pane, and Search Results window. This can increase your productivity by displaying only the required file property information in an easy-to-view display.

The **Customize View** option is available when you right-click on a column heading, as shown in Figure 7–5.

*The **Customize View** option is also available when you right-click in any white space in the Main table or Preview pane.*

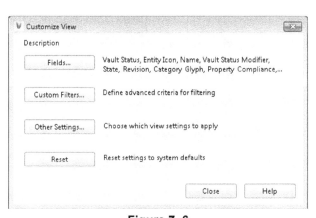

Figure 7–5

When you select **Customize View**, the Customize View dialog box opens as shown in Figure 7–6. The options available vary depending on whether you click **Customize View** in the Main table, Preview pane, and Search Results window.

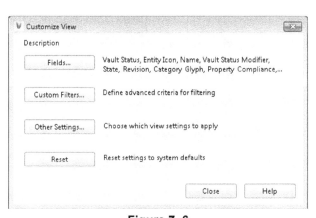

Figure 7–6

Column Display

To customize the columns that display, click **Fields...** in the Customize View dialog box. The Customize Fields dialog box opens. The *Show these fields in this order* area contains the columns that are currently displayed and their display order, as shown in Figure 7–7.

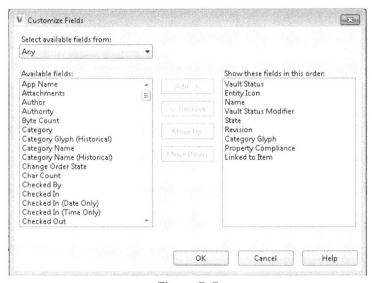

Figure 7–7

Adding Columns

You can add columns to the Main table and customize the order in which they display.

How To: Add Columns to the Main Table

1. In the Customize Fields dialog box, in the Select available fields from drop-down list, select one of the options as shown in Figure 7–8.

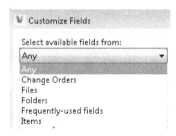

Figure 7–8

2. In the *Available fields* area, select a property as shown in Figure 7–9. Click **Add** to move the property to the *Show these fields in this order* area.

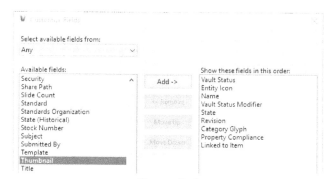

Figure 7–9

3. Click **OK**.

Changing Column Order

In the Customize Fields dialog box, the order in which the columns are shown is the order in which they display in the Main table.

How To: Change the Column Order

You can also change the column order by dragging and dropping a column heading to a new position in the Main table.

1. In the Customize Fields dialog box, in the *Show these fields in this order* area, select the property field to reorder.
2. Click **Move Up** to move the property field up (i.e., to the left in the Main table). Click **Move Down** to move the property field down (i.e., to the right in the Main table).
3. Click **OK**.

Removing Columns

You can remove columns from the Main table.

How To: Remove a Column

1. In the Customize Fields dialog box, in the *Show these fields in this order* area, select the property to remove.
2. Click **Remove**. You can also remove a column by selecting a column heading, right-clicking, and selecting **Remove This Column**.
3. Click **OK**.

Text Alignment

You can modify the alignment of the text displayed in the columns in the Main table.

How To: Align the Text in a Column

1. Select the column heading, right-click on **Alignment** to display the alignment options as shown in Figure 7–10.

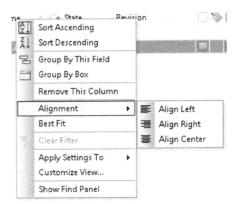

Figure 7–10

2. Select the required type of alignment: **Align Left**, **Align Right**, or **Align Center**. The text in the column updates accordingly.

Column Size

You can modify the width of the columns in the Main table.

How To: Resize a Column

1. Hover over the right edge of the column heading border so that the double arrowheads display (↔).
2. Drag the border to manually resize the column.

You can also resize columns as follows:

- Select the column heading, right-click, and select **Best Fit** to automatically resize the column to fit the data.

- Double-click on the right edge of the column heading border to automatically fit the column width to the data.

Sorting

You can sort the data that displays in the columns in the Main table.

How To: Sort Data in a Column

You can also select the column heading to switch between the ascending and descending sort type.

1. Select the column heading, right-click, and select **Sort Ascending** or **Sort Descending**.

   - **Sort Ascending:** Sorts columns from A to Z, reading from top to bottom (or from the lowest to highest number). If a column is sorted in ascending order, an up arrow displays in the column heading, as shown in Figure 7–11.

   - **Sort Descending:** Sorts columns from Z to A, reading from top to bottom (or from the highest to lowest number). If a column is sorted in descending order, a down arrow displays in the column heading as shown in Figure 7–12.

| Figure 7–11 | Figure 7–12 |

Grouping

You can sort the contents of the Main table and Preview pane by any combination of column headings. Objects that have the same values for the selected properties are then listed together. For example, you can group a folder by designer, version, date, etc. for a more manageable view of the folder.

How To: Group by Column Headings

1. Select the column heading, right-click, and select **Group By This Field**. The column heading is moved to the *Group By Box* area and the contents are grouped and collapsed, as shown in Figure 7–13.

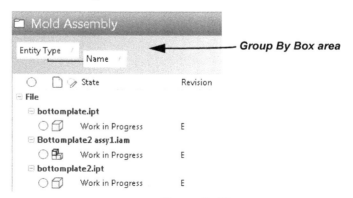

Figure 7–13

You can also drag the column heading next to the first one in the Group By Box area to add a sub-group. Drag it back to the other column headings to remove the sub-group.

⬚ (Group By Box) is also located in the Advanced toolbar.

2. If you need to place another group in the first one (a sub-group), right-click on another column heading, and select **Group By This Field**.
3. To expand all of the groups, right-click in the *Group By Box* area, and select **Full Expand**.
4. To collapse all of the groups, right-click in the *Group By Box* area, and select **Full Collapse**.
5. To clear the group so that the files display as a flat list without any groups, right-click in the *Group By Box* area, and select **Clear Grouping**.
6. To remove the *Group By Box* area, right-click on a column heading, and select **Group By Box** to toggle it off.

Additional Settings

Additional settings can be found by clicking **Other Settings...** in the Customize View dialog box. The settings are shown in Figure 7–14.

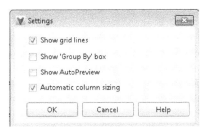

Figure 7–14

Filters

You can hide contents based on specific criteria by defining column filters.

How To: Create a column filter

*Filters can also be created by clicking **Custom Filters...** in the Customize View dialog box.*

1. In the Main table or Preview pane, hover the cursor over a column heading. A filter icon displays, as shown in Figure 7–15.

Figure 7–15

2. Click the filter icon and select a filter in the drop-down list to apply to the column. Some of the available filters include:
   - **(Custom):** Opens the Custom Auto Filter dialog box so that a custom filter can be created.
   - **Column Values:** Displays data for the selected file.
3. To create a custom filter, select **(Custom)**.

4. In the *Name* area, expand the drop-down list and select an operator as shown in Figure 7–16.

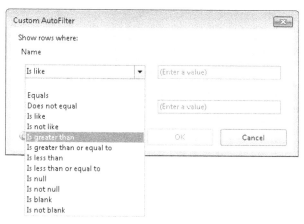

Figure 7–16

5. Enter a value for the file property.
6. You can specify up to two types of search criteria. Select **And** to combine the criteria or select **Or** to contain either criteria.
7. Click **OK** to complete the custom filter definition and display the results. The line at the bottom of the pane indicates that a custom filter is being used, as shown in Figure 7–17.

Figure 7–17

*The filter can also be removed by right-clicking on the column heading, and selecting **Clear Filter**.*

8. When a filter is created, you can temporarily toggle it off or remove it. To toggle off a filter, click ☑ at the bottom of the Main table list. To remove the filter, click ☒. Toggling off or removing a filter causes the complete list of files to be displayed. Click ▾ to select from the list of available filters.

Reset Current View

To reset the column view to the default configuration, click **Reset** in the Customize View dialog box.

7.3 Custom Views

Custom views enable you to create your own configuration of the interface. Once created, you can modify, rename, copy, delete, or reuse it.

How To: Create a Custom View

1. In the Advanced toolbar, expand the drop-down list and select **Define custom views...** as shown in Figure 7–18.

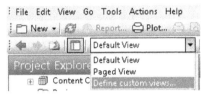

Figure 7–18

2. In the Manage Custom Views dialog box, click **New...**.
3. For *View Name*, enter a name for the custom view and click **OK**.
4. In the Manage Custom Views dialog box, click **Modify...**.
5. In the Customize View dialog box, click **Fields...**.
6. In the Customize Fields dialog box, select the columns that you want to display in the custom view.
7. Click **Close** to close the dialog box and apply the settings.

7.4 Shortcuts

Shortcuts can be used to quickly access specific folders or objects. When the shortcut is selected, the associated folder or object displays in the Main table. Vault shortcuts can also be accessed in the Autodesk Inventor Open and Place From Vault dialog boxes for quick retrieval of components and designs.

When created, shortcuts are added to the My Shortcuts pane, which is part of the Navigation pane. The My Shortcuts pane is hidden when the Navigation pane is hidden but can also be hidden independent of the Navigation pane. To hide the My Shortcuts pane, clear the **View>Shortcuts Pane** option.

Shortcuts can be renamed, organized by groups, and removed. Shortcut groups can be created to organize your shortcuts for quick and easy access.

Create Shortcut

You can create shortcuts to quickly access frequently used folders or objects.

How To: Create a Shortcut

1. In the Navigation pane or Main table, select a folder or file.
2. Right-click and select **Create Shortcut**. A shortcut displays in the My Shortcuts pane, as shown in Figure 7–19. In this example, a shortcut was created to the *Hub Shaft* folder and to the **Operating instructions.doc** file.

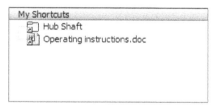

Figure 7–19

3. To rename a shortcut, right-click on it and select **Rename**. Enter a new name.
4. To remove a shortcut, right-click on it and select **Delete**. Only the shortcut is removed and not the associated folder or object.

Create Shortcut Groups

You can organize your shortcuts using groups to make them easier to locate.

How To: Create a Shortcut Group

1. In the My Shortcuts pane, right-click and select **New Group**. Enter a name for the group.
2. Drag existing shortcuts to the new group and drag them in the group to change their order. An example of a group is shown in Figure 7–20.

Figure 7–20

3. To rename a shortcut group, right-click on it and select **Rename**. Enter a new name.
4. To remove a shortcut group, right-click on it and select **Delete**. This also removes any shortcuts in the group.

Practice 7a

Customizing the User Interface

Practice Objectives

- Use the View menu and Customize View option to customize the Autodesk Vault window.
- Apply a filter to the main table.
- Create a shortcut.

In this practice, you will customize the user interface to display only the Main table and thumbnail images in the Main table. You will also use a filter to hide .BMP files in the Main table and add a frequently accessed assembly to the Shortcut pane.

Task 1 - Toggle off the Navigation and Preview panes.

In this task, you will toggle off the Navigation and Preview panes so that only the Main table displays.

1. In the Autodesk Vault software, select the *Hub Shaft* folder.

2. Select **View>Navigation Pane** and **View>Preview Pane** so that these panes are no longer displayed.

Task 2 - Add a new column field to the Main table.

In this task, you will add a new column to the Main table so that you can display a thumbnail image.

1. In the Main table, right-click on a column heading and select **Customize View**.

2. In the Customize View dialog box, click **Fields...**.

3. In the Customize Fields dialog box, expand the Select available fields from drop-down list, and select **Files**.

4. In the *Available fields* area, select **Thumbnail** and click **Add** to add it to the *Show these fields in this order* area.

5. In the *Show these fields in this order* area, select **Thumbnail** and click **Move Up** so that it is first in the list. Click **OK**.

6. Click **Close** to close the Customize View dialog box and complete the change. The thumbnail images display in the first column for each applicable file in the Main table, as shown in Figure 7–21.

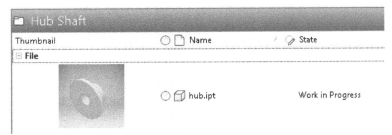

Figure 7–21

Task 3 - Adjust the Name column.

1. Double-click on the border on the right side of the *Name* column heading to adjust the column size to fit the data.

2. Click the *Name* column to sort the list of files alphabetically, in ascending order.

Task 4 - Apply a filter to the Main table.

In this task, you will create a custom filter to exclude all .BMP files from the display.

1. Select **View>Navigation Pane** to display the Navigation pane.

2. Select the *Vise* folder.

3. Identify the *sample rendered image.bmp* file. This is the file that you will filter out of the display.

4. Hover the cursor over the *Name* column and click ⬇. In the drop-down list, select **(Custom)**.

5. In the Custom AutoFilter dialog box, select the **Is not like** operator.

6. For the condition, type ***.bmp**.

Once a filter is created, it is available for use in all folders.

7. Click **OK**. The .BMP file is removed from the display and the filter displays at the bottom of the pane, as shown in Figure 7–22. You can disable the filter by clearing the checkmark.

Figure 7–22

Task 5 - Undo/delete the customizations.

In this task, you will undo the user interface customizations.

1. Select **View>Preview Pane** to toggle on the Preview pane.

2. To delete the thumbnail image from the Main table, select the Thumbnail column heading, right-click, and select **Remove This Column**.

3. Click [X] at the bottom of the Main table to remove the filter and see the *rendered image.bmp* file return to the list.

Task 6 - Add a shortcut.

1. Select **vise.iam**, right-click, and select **Create Shortcut** to add the assembly to the My Shortcuts pane, as shown in Figure 7–23. You can also drag the file to the My Shortcuts pane. If the My Shortcuts pane is not displayed, click **View>Shortcuts Pane**.

Figure 7–23

Chapter Review Questions

1. In the Autodesk Vault interface, what are some of the ways in which you can customize the window display? (Select all that apply.)

   a. You can toggle on and off the Navigation and Preview panes.

   b. You can apply a filter to a column to only display objects with specified file formats, for example.

   c. You can change the font size in the main table.

   d. You can resize and reorder the columns.

2. How can you resize columns to fit the data? (Select all that apply.)

   a. Drag the border to manually resize the column.

   b. Select the column heading, right-click, and select **Alignment**.

   c. Select the column heading, right-click, and select **Best Fit** to automatically resize the column to fit the data.

   d. Double-click on the right edge of the column heading border to automatically fit the column width to the data.

3. How do you remove a filter? (Select all that apply.)

   a. Click ⊠ at the bottom of the Main table list next to the filter.

   b. Select the column heading, right-click, and select **Clear Filter**.

   c. Click ☐ at the bottom of the Main table list to place a checkmark for the filter.

   d. Click **Reset** in the Customize View dialog box.

4. When you remove a shortcut, you also remove the associated folder or object?

   a. True

   b. False

Command Summary

Button	Command	Location
	Auto Preview	• Advanced Toolbar
	Group By Box	• Advanced Toolbar
	Preview Pane	• Advanced Toolbar

Chapter

8

File and Design Management

One of the Autodesk® Vault software's key features is its ability to consolidate and manage all product information for easy reference, sharing, and reuse. In this chapter, you learn about managing files in the vault, editing object properties and the Copy Design tool. The Copy Design tool copies an entire design, including all related files, while maintaining their relationships to each other in the new design file.

Learning Objectives in this Chapter

- Use the Move, Delete, and Attachments operations to move, delete, and attach files to other files in the vault.
- Use the Edit Properties operation to edit object properties.
- Create a label to capture a project milestone
- Use the Rename operation to rename files and update all related files that reference the renamed files.
- Use the Replace operation to replace files with new files and update the parent references.
- Use the Pack and Go command to copy all referenced files to a single location outside the Autodesk Inventor software.
- Use Workspace Sync to clean up files in your project workspace.
- Use the Copy Design operation to create a new design.

8.1 Managing Data in the Vault

Autodesk Vault's data management functionality includes the ability to move, delete, rename, and attach files to other files in the vault.

To ensure file resolution when performing data management operations, the project specified in Autodesk Inventor's Project Settings is used. An administrator can set up an Autodesk Inventor project file to be used for all of the clients. If you are not an administrator, you can specify the Autodesk Inventor project file in the Autodesk Vault software by selecting **Tools>Options** or by right-clicking on the project file and selecting **Set Inventor Project File,** as shown in Figure 8–1.

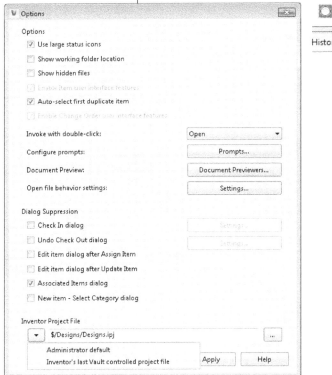
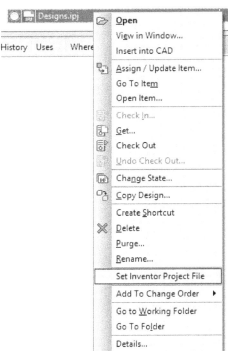

Figure 8–1

Moving Files

You can also move a file by dragging and dropping it into its new folder using the left mouse button.

To move files from one folder to another, select the files in the Main table, hold the right mouse button, and drag them into the target folder. When you release the right mouse button after dragging, select **Move** as shown in Figure 8–2.

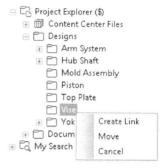

Figure 8–2

The file remains the same in the new location and is still referenced by its children and parents.

Deleting Files

To delete vault files, select them in the Main table, right-click, and select **Delete**. You are prompted to confirm the action. The **Delete** operation deletes all versions of the selected files. You can also delete files by clicking ✖ (Delete) in the Main toolbar or selecting **Edit>Delete**.

When using the **Delete** operation:

- Parents need to be deleted before children.

- A file must be in a **Checked In** state.

- If a file label exists, it needs to be deleted before the file is deleted.

Attaching Files to Other Files

Files can be attached to other files in the vault, which creates a link between the files so that they act as a unit when being checked out and checked in. For example, you might want to attach a Microsoft Word document containing operating instructions to a design file.

How To: Attach a File to Another File

1. In the Main table, select the files to which you want to attach a file and select **Actions>Attachments**.
2. Click **Attach...** and select the files to attach.
3. Click **OK**.

Attachments display with a paper clip symbol, in the *Uses* tab, as shown for **yoke.ipt** in Figure 8–3.

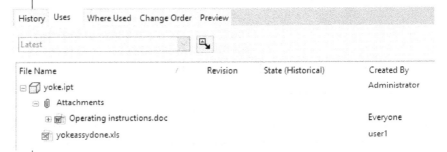

Figure 8–3

How To: Remove Attachments from a File

1. In the Main table, select the file from which you want to remove an attachment and select **Actions>Attachments**.
2. Select the attachment filename and click **Detach**.
3. Click **OK**.

8.2 Properties

Editing Properties

The Autodesk Vault software includes both System-Defined Properties and User-Defined Properties (UDPs). The **Edit Properties** command in the Autodesk Vault software enables you to edit User Defined Properties of selected objects, such as files, items, and change orders. When updating file properties, files are automatically checked out and then checked back in to the vault with the file property updates.

Your user role must be defined as Editor or Administrator to edit file properties. Items can only be edited by an Item Editor Level 1, Item Editor Level 2, or an Administrator.

You can also select multiple object types for editing.

How To: Edit File Properties

1. In the Autodesk Vault software main table view, with the objects selected, select **Edit>Edit Properties**. Alternatively, with the objects selected, in the Properties grid, click

   ✐ (Edit Properties).
2. The Property Edit dialog box opens displaying the objects to edit. You can add additional objects or remove any objects using **Add** and **Remove**, respectively. By default, the properties of **Name**, **Author**, and **Description** display.
   - Properties that display with a gray background are read-only.
   - Properties that display with a white background can be edited. Double-click the property and type a new value.

3. Click ▯▯▯ (Select Properties) to add more properties.
4. In the Customize Fields dialog box, in the *Select available fields from* drop-down list, select one of the following options to determine the type of properties to be displayed: **All fields**, **Files**, **Folders**, or **Frequently-used fields**.
5. In the *Available fields* area, select a property.
6. Click **Add** to add the property to the *Show these fields in this order* area.
7. In the *Show these fields in this order* area, use **Move Up** or **Move Down** to organize the properties.
8. In the *Show these fields in this order* area, use **Remove** to remove a property from the list.
9. Click **OK**.

The new value for a file property must be the appropriate data type or it displays as incorrect.

10. Edit the properties by double-clicking on a cell and changing its value. You can also right-click on a cell to access the **Copy**, **Paste**, **Select All**, **Capitalize**, **Find**, and **Replace** options, as shown in Figure 8–4.

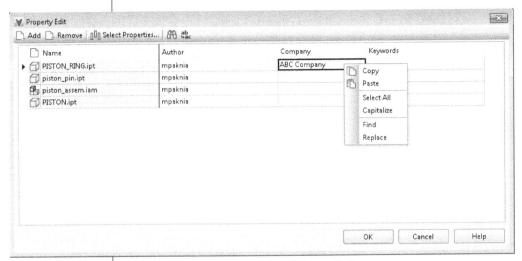

Figure 8–4

11. Drag the small black square at the bottom right corner of the selected cell to fill the other cells with the same value.
12. Click **OK**.
13. The Property Edit Results dialog box opens displaying the updated properties as shown in Figure 8–5.

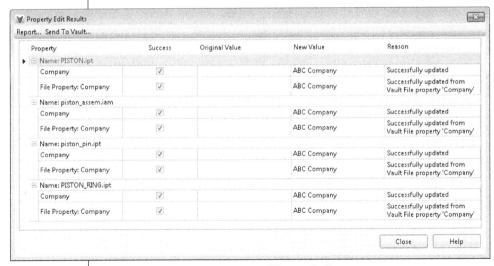

Figure 8–5

14. Select **Report** to print or export the results. The Preview window enables you to use the following options to modify, print, or export the report:

    - Add a header or footer, adjust the margins, and set the display to **Portrait** or **Landscape**.
    - Add a watermark or change the color of the background.
    - Export the report as a .PDF, .HTML, .MHT, .RTF, .XLS, .XLSX, .CSV, .TXT, or image file.
    - Send the report via email.
    - Customize how the report is going to print by selecting which items are going to print (header, footer, lines, etc.) and how the report is going to fit on the printed page.

15. In the Property Edits Results dialog box, select **Send To Vault** to save the report in the vault. In the Save As dialog box, select the vault in which to save the report, enter the report name, and click **Save**.

16. Click **Close**. The *Comment* field displays **Property Edit** to explain the version change for files with modified properties.

Creating UDPs

How To: Create a New User Defined Property

1. Click **Tools>Administration>Vault Settings**.
2. Select the *Behaviors* tab and click **Properties**.
3. In the Property Definitions dialog box, click **New**.
4. In the New Property dialog box, enter a name.
5. In the Type drop-down list, select the property type, as shown in Figure 8–6.

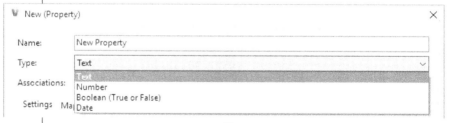

Figure 8–6

6. Assign the UDP to one or more categories by selecting the category checkboxes in the Associations drop-down list, as shown in Figure 8–7.

- Categories can be preselected in this list based on the filter you selected previously in the Property Definitions dialog box.
- You can select or clear categories as required.

Figure 8–7

Add or Remove Properties

How To: Add or Remove Properties from Files or Items

1. Select the required objects and then select **Actions>Add or Remove Property**.
2. Locate the property and select **Add** or **Remove** from the Action drop-down list, as shown in Figure 8–8.

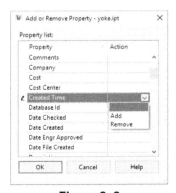

Figure 8–8

8.3 Labels

In the Autodesk Vault software, labels can be created to capture project milestones, such as customer proposals and design reviews. They act as snapshots of your data at a specific point in the design process. You can assign specific documents to these labels. Once the label has been created, you can use the **Pack and Go** operation to create a package based on that label. You can also roll back the design based on a label.

How To: Create a Label

1. Select **Tools>Labels**. The Labels dialog box opens as shown in Figure 8–9.

Figure 8–9

The Labels dialog box displays the list of labels that have already been defined and enables labels to be created, deleted, renamed, archived, and restored. It displays the *Created By* and *Create Date* information on a label, the number of files assigned to it, and any associated comments.

*You can also create a new label by selecting a vault folder, right-clicking, and selecting **New Label**.*

2. In the Labels dialog box, click **New...** to create a new label. The New Label dialog box opens as shown in Figure 8–10.

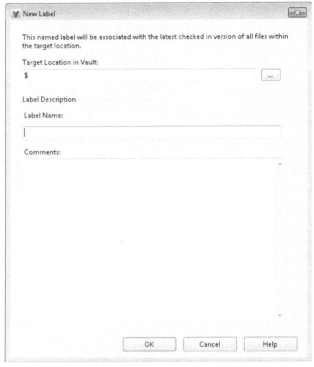

Figure 8–10

There is no limit to the number of labels that can be assigned to a project.
*Label names must be unique in the database and can contain any alphanumeric text, excluding \ / : * ? " < > |*

3. Select the target location for the label. The latest version of all of the files at that location is assigned that label. If child references exist outside the specified location, those files are also assigned that label.
4. Enter the name of the label that indicates the milestone. Since the folder information is not included, it is a good idea to include it in the name.
5. Enter comments that clearly summarize the content of the label.
6. Click **OK**.

Editing a Label

To edit a label, select one from the list and click **Edit...**. Enter a new name or edit the comments and click **OK**.

Deleting a Label

To delete a label, select a label from the list and click **Delete**. Click **Yes** to confirm deletion.

Extracting a Label

To extract a label, select a label from the list and click **Pack and Go** to create a package of the label contents. Specify the Pack and Go details, as shown in Figure 8–11, including selecting which label to retrieve.

Figure 8–11

Restoring

When restoring a label, the version of the file associated to the label becomes the current version To restore a label, select one from the list and click **Restore**. Click **Yes** to confirm the restore and creation of the new version.

8.4 Rename Wizard

Your user role must be defined as Editor or Administrator to use the Rename Wizard.

The **Rename** operation in the Autodesk Vault software uses the Rename Wizard. In addition to renaming files, this operation updates all related files that reference the renamed files to ensure that all relationships remain intact. You must have permission to check out the files. Any file in the vault can be renamed using the Rename Wizard, except for .DWF files which are automatically published.

How To: Use the Rename Wizard

You can also select a file and then select Edit>Rename.

1. In the Autodesk Vault software, select the files, right-click, and select **Rename**. The Rename Wizard opens listing the files to be renamed and their vault folders. You can add or remove files in this page.
2. Click **Next>**. The Rename Wizard dialog box displays all related files and their vault locations that are affected by the name change.
3. Click **Next>**. Enter the new name for each file in the list, as shown in Figure 8–12.

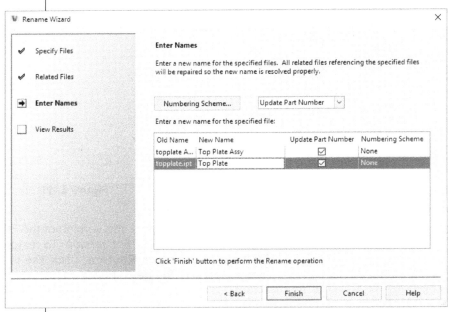

Figure 8–12

4. Select the checkbox in the *Update Part Number* column if you want to assign the new filename to the Part Number iProperty for Autodesk Inventor files.
5. Click **Finish**. The Rename Wizard performs the operation and displays the results.
6. Click **Save...** to export the results. Select the folder in which to save the report, enter the report name, and click **Save...**
7. Click **Send to Vault...** to save the report in the vault. Select the vault in which to save the report, enter the report name, and click **Save...**.
8. Click **Close**.

8.5 Replace Wizard

The Replace Wizard enables you to replace files with new files, which automatically updates the parent references. A new version of the parent that references the new file is created.

How To: Use the Replace Wizard

1. In the Autodesk Vault software, select the files, and select **Edit>Replace**. The Replace Wizard dialog box opens listing the files to be replaced and their vault folders. You can add or remove files from this page.
2. Click **Next>**.
3. In the Related Files page, all parent files display by default. To exclude a parent file from being updated with the new reference, clear the associated option.
4. Click **Next>**.
5. In the Specify Replacement Files page shown in Figure 8–13, click [...] (Browse) to select a new file to replace the old file. Do this for each listed file.

Replace can also be accomplished using the ***Copy Design*** *option.*

The status of the new file that replaces the old file does not matter.

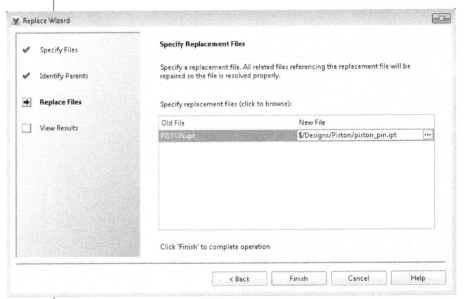

Figure 8–13

6. Click **Finish**. The Replace Wizard performs the operation and displays the results.
7. Click **Save...** to export the results to a text file.
8. Click **Save...** to save the report in the vault as shown in Figure 8–14. Select the vault in which to save the report, enter the report name, and click **Save...**.

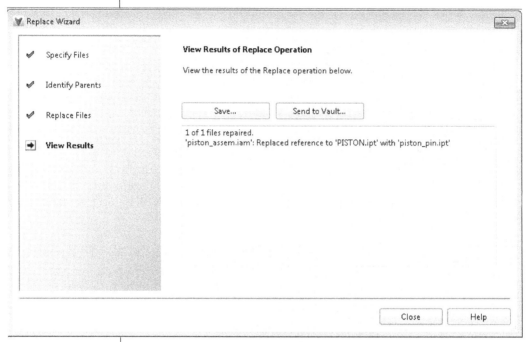

Figure 8–14

9. Click **Close**.

8.6 Pack and Go

An Autodesk Inventor assembly or drawing can reference multiple parts, assemblies, and presentation files. The **Pack and Go** tool enables you to copy all of the referenced files to a single location outside of the Autodesk Inventor software, while also maintaining links to the referenced files. **Pack and Go** can be accessed from the Autodesk Inventor software, the Windows Explorer, or the Autodesk Vault software.

The **Pack and Go** tool is useful for archiving files, isolating a design for experimentation, and providing a complete project to a vendor who might not have access to the Autodesk Vault software. When using **Pack and Go**, you can specify the version of the files to retrieve, and whether you want to keep the folder hierarchy.

In addition, the **Pack and Go** tool can make it easier to add Autodesk Inventor projects that reside outside the vault. It creates a single-user project file that can then be converted into a vault project for use in the vault.

How To: Package a File and its References in Autodesk Vault

1. In the Autodesk Vault software, select the file that you want to package.
2. Select **File>Pack and Go**. All of the files referenced by the selected file display as shown in Figure 8–15.

Figure 8–15

3. Set the *Package Type* option to one of the following:
   - **Zip file (*.zip)**
   - **Unzipped**
   - **DWF Package**
   - **DWFx Package**
4. Set the *Send To* option to one of the following:
   - **Destination Folder**
   - **Mail Recipient**
   - **SharePoint Directory**
5. Set the *Revision to Get* option to the revision you want to package (**Latest**).
6. Set the *Output Structure* option to one of the following:
   - **Copy to Single Path**
   - **Keep Folder Hierarchy**
7. Click ⊟ (Settings). In the Settings dialog box, in the *Children (uses)* and *Other relationships* areas, select one of the following options:
   - **Include dependents**
   - **Include attachments**
   - **Include library files**
   - **Include related documentation**
8. In the Settings dialog box, in the *Visualization Filter* area, select one of the following options:
   - **Include Visualization Files**
   - **Exclude Visualization Files**
   - **Visualization Files Only**
9. Click **OK**. If **Mail Recipient** was selected in the *Send To* field, an email message opens. Depending on the Package Type selected, you are prompted for a folder or filename.

How To: Package a File and its References in Windows Explorer

1. In Windows Explorer, right-click on the file you want to package and select **Pack and Go**. The Pack and Go dialog box opens. Click **More>>** to display the entire dialog box, as shown in Figure 8–16.

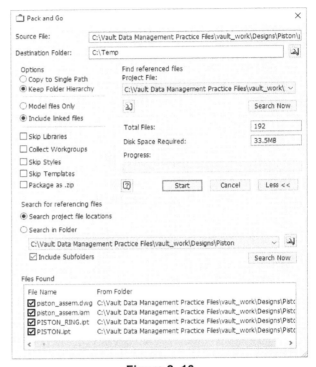

Figure 8–16

2. Click ![Browse icon] (Browse) and select the destination folder.
3. In the *Options* area, select the options for:
   - Controlling the folder structure,
   - Whether to include only Autodesk Inventor files or all linked files (spreadsheets, etc.), and
   - Whether to skip libraries, templates, and styles or to collect workgroups.
4. In the *Find referenced files* area, set the *Project File* by selecting a project from the drop-down list, or by clicking

   ![Select project icon] (Select project to use) and browsing to the project file.

Referenced files are typically drawing or presentation files.

5. In the *Find referenced files* area, click **Search Now**. The child files are listed in the *Files Found* area.
6. In the *Search for referencing files* area, click **Search Now**. Any files referencing the selected files are listed in the dialog box, which enables you to select which files to add to the list.
7. Click **Start** to begin copying the files.
8. When the process is complete, click **Done** to close the Pack and Go dialog box.

8.7 Synchronize Your Workspace

You can synchronize the contents of your local workspace with the corresponding Vault folders. This operation either updates the files in either location, or removes files from the workspace.

You can click **Workspace Sync** to manually select the local files to synchronize and select the Settings for additional options. Alternatively, you can select **Quick Sync** from the drop-down menu to synchronize immediately using the default settings.

How To: Synchronize your Workspace

1. Select **Workspace Sync** from the toolbar, as shown in Figure 8–17.

Figure 8–17

2. Select the checkboxes for the files you would like to synchronize, as shown in Figure 8–18. Removed files are placed in the Windows Recycle Bin.

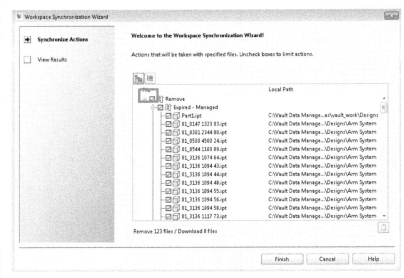

Figure 8–18

3. Select **Finish**. The results display as shown in Figure 8–19.

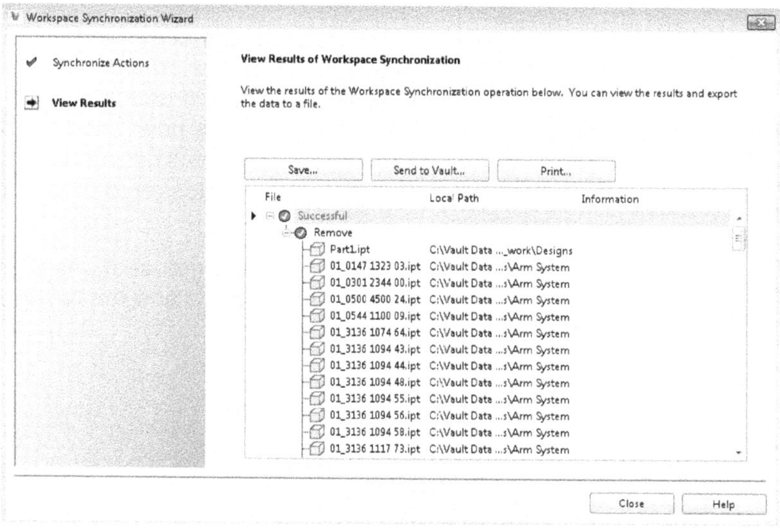

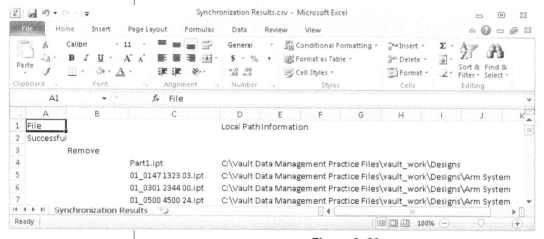

Figure 8–19

4. If you would like to save the results to a .CSV file, click **Save** to save the file to a specified folder, or click **Send to Vault** to save the file to a Vault folder. An example of a .CSV file is shown in Figure 8–20.

Figure 8–20

8.8 Copy Design

The **Copy Design** command enables you to copy an entire design (including all related files, parts, drawings, subassemblies, and attachments), and maintain their relationships to the new design. **Copy Design** commands can include copying, reusing, replacing, and excluding specified files from the existing design to create the new design.

Copy Design Interface

There are three major sections of the Copy Design interface: the Toolbar, Main View, and the Navigation Panel, as shown in Figure 8–21.

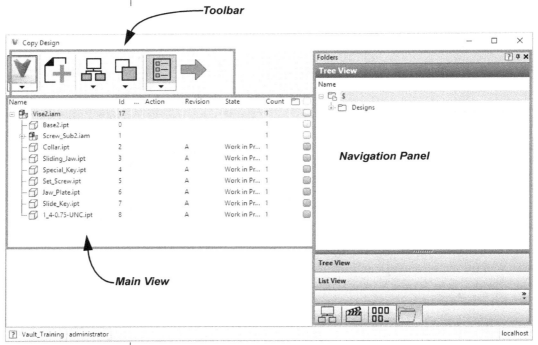

Figure 8–21

The Tool Bar

Use the toolbar to log in and out of a vault, access administrative options, add objects to the main view, control copy settings or rule sets, and create copies.

Icons and Details	Sub-Menus
Master Menu Log In... Log Out... Refresh Drawing View Select References ☑ Automatically Copy Parents ☑ Link Drawings and Model Action Rules... Numbering Schemes... Panels ▸ About...	**Log In** Log in to a vault to access designs for copying. **Log Out** Log out of a vault when you are finished or when you want to switch to a different vault.
Add Objects	Add the files that you want to copy to the main view with **Add Objects**.
Include Children	By default, all library files and attachments are set to copy. However you can assign different copy actions to children files by displaying them in the Copy Design view. Use **Include Children** to toggle whether children files display in the Copy Design view. Select which types of children files to show by selecting one or both of the following check-boxes: • **Attachments:** Displays all file attachments. **Note:** All file formats are shown, including generic file attachments. • **Include Library Files:** Displays all associated library files.
Select Copy Settings	• **Copy Top Nodes**: You can copy multiple design trees with one command. Selecting **Copy Top Nodes** sets all top level components to copy. • **Copy All**: Select Copy All to designate all files in the main view for copy.

Select Rule Set	A Rule set determines the file properties and settings for copied files when certain conditions are met.
	Users can select from a list of existing rule sets. The Rule Set sub-menu lists all of the existing rule sets.
	If no rule set is selected, the target file receives the same file properties and settings as the source file.
Create Copy	Once everything is configured, click Create Copy to begin the copy operation.

The Main View Grid

The main Copy Design view shows the name of the files available to copy, the file identification number, the action that will be performed on the file, the revision and state of the file, and how many instances (Count) of the file occur in the current list.

Tip: By default, reference filenames are set to the destination filename when an action is assigned. You can view the Numbering Panel to identify files by their original name, or add File Name (Historical) to the main view.

You can also manage copy actions and customize the view from the main view, as shown in Figure 8–22.

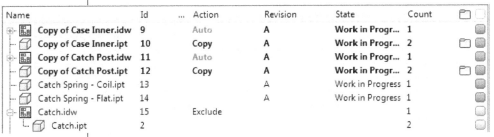

Name	Id	...	Action	Revision	State	Count		
Copy of Case Inner.idw	9		Auto	A	Work in Progr...	1		
Copy of Case Inner.ipt	10		Copy	A	Work in Progr...	2		
Copy of Catch Post.idw	11		Auto	A	Work in Progr...	1		
Copy of Catch Post.ipt	12		Copy	A	Work in Progr...	2		
Catch Spring - Coil.ipt	13			A	Work in Progress	1		
Catch Spring - Flat.ipt	14			A	Work in Progress	1		
Catch.idw	15		Exclude			1		
Catch.ipt	2					2		

Figure 8–22

To change a copy action, select the file, right-click and select **Copy**, **Copy To...**, **Replace...**, **Exclude** or **Reuse**. **Copy To...** and **Replace...** prompt you to select the destination folder and replacement file, respectively.

The available file operations depend on the type of file selected. These are described as follows:

Operation	Description
Copy	Generates a new file that is independent of the selected source file.
Copy To...	Enables you to change the destination folder of the selected file.
Reuse	Keeps the selected file in the new design while maintaining all links.
Exclude	Omits the selected file from the new design.
Replace...	Enables you to substitute the selected file with another one.

The Navigation Panel

There are four different navigation panels, each located on their own tab:

- Where Used

- Actions

- Numbering

- Folders

The Actions panel is shown with its tab selected as shown in Figure 8–23.

Figure 8–23

The options available in the four navigation panels is as follows.

Panel	Details
Where Used	The Where Used panel lets users track the origin of the copy objects and their destination.
	Since you can replace existing files with uncommitted instances of files that are being copied, this means that the copied instance can have numerous destinations. Use the Where Used tab to ensure that the files are copied to the correct locations.
Actions	The Actions Panel enables you to review which operations are going to be performed on files in the main view.
	Once you have configured the files in the main view, you can use the Actions Panel to filter the files based on their assigned operation. Assigned operations include copied, reused, replaced, excluded, or edited.
	Use the Actions Panel to verify the copy design configuration in the main view and to make changes.
	Note that you can also set Action operations by dragging and dropping files from the main grid onto the required operation button in the Actions Panel.

Numbering	The Numbering Panel lists all of the files selected for copying. It also shows the original and new name for each selected file.
	The grid displays the renaming options based on available numbering schemes.
	In the Numbering Panel grid, you can edit certain fields and individual numbering schemes.
Folders	The Folders Panel enables you to review the source and destination folders for the copy design operation. This helps you verify that the required files are selected and are being copied to the correct location.
	You can group selected files for operations based on the folder location. You can also drag-and-drop files between folders or from the main grid to perform a copy. You can also display the files in a Tree View or List View. There is **Find and Replace** functionality in the List View, in the shortcut menu, as shown below.

```
Select All
View                    ▶
Choose Columns...
Refresh
Find and Replace...
```

How To: Perform a Copy Design

1. Select and right-click on a file from the main table and then select **Copy Design**. Alternatively, you can find the Copy Design command through the Start menu under **Autodesk Data Management>Tools**.
2. If you are not already logged in, you are prompted to log in to a vault. Enter your credentials and click **OK**.
3. Expand ⚘ on the toolbar and select which of the following options you want to be enabled
   - Drawing View
   - Select References
   - Automatically Copy Parents
   - Link Drawings and Model

   Note: You can also access Action Rules, Numbering Schemes, and Panels Configuration from this menu.

4. Click (Add Objects). Select the files that you want to copy and then click **Open**. The files are added to the main view of the Copy Design dialog.

5. Click (Include Children) and select whether you want to show Attachments, Library Files, or both in the copy design view.

6. If required, click (Select Copy Settings) and select whether you want to copy only the top nodes or all of the files listed in the main view.

7. If you want to perform a different action on a file, right-click on the file and select the action from the context menu.

   - **Tip:** Click **Refresh** at any time to capture the latest version of the listed files and file structure.

8. Click (Rule Set) and select the rule set that you want to apply to the copy operation.

   - **Note:** Toggle Rule Set off to ignore rule sets for this copy operation. All source file properties are applied to the destination files. If configured, category and numbering schemes are also applied to the destination files. However, the state and revision of the destination file are always reset.

9. Once everything is configured, click (Create Copy) to start the copy operation.

Once you start the copy operation, several prechecks are performed to ensure the following:

- All files have unique names (by Folder).

- Vault unique filename rules are met.

- Selected files still exist.

- Files requiring edits are write-enabled.

- Files requiring edits are owned by the workgroup site.

All successful copy operations receive a green checkmark in the main view. If a copy operation failed, a red cross displays. To perform another copy operation, modify your settings and click Create Copy.

Practice 8a

Data Management and Rename Wizard

Practice Objectives

- Use the Move operation.
- Attach one file to another.
- Rename an assembly and a part.

In this practice, you will use Autodesk Vault's file management functionality to move and rename files. In addition, you will attach a file to another file to have them behave as one unit.

Task 1 - Set the Autodesk Inventor project file.

1. In the Main table of the Autodesk Vault software, in the $\Designs folder, locate **Designs.ipj**.

You can also set the Autodesk Inventor project file in Autodesk Vault by selecting **Tools>Options**.

2. Right-click **Designs.ipj** and select **Set Inventor Project File,** as shown in Figure 8–24.

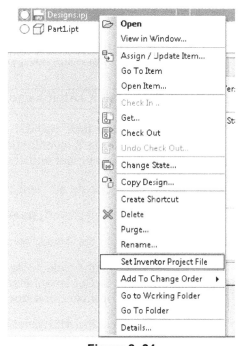

Figure 8–24

Task 2 - Move a file from one folder to another.

1. Locate the file **3136 1094 44.ipt**.

2. In the Search Results, right-click on the file and select **Go To Folder**. It is located in the $*Designs\Arm System* folder and is being used in three assemblies as shown in the Where Used tab of the Preview Pane (**3136 1133 82.iam**, **Middle Arm-N.iam**, and **Arm System.iam**) as shown in Figure 8–25.

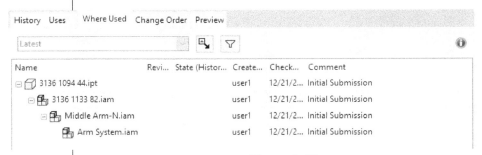

Figure 8–25

3. In the Main table, select **3136 1094 44.ipt** and drag it into the $*Designs\Yoke* folder.

4. In the $*Designs\Yoke* folder, select **3136 1094 44.ipt**. In the Preview pane, select the *Where Used* tab to see that it maintains the child relationships to the three assemblies.

Task 3 - Attach one file to another.

In this task, you will attach a Microsoft Word document to an Autodesk Inventor part file so that they behave as one unit when checking out and checking in.

1. Locate and select **yoke.ipt**.

2. Select **Actions>Attachments**.

3. In the Attachments dialog box, click **Attach...**.

4. In the Select File to Attach dialog box, in the $>*Documentation* folder, locate and select the file **Operating instructions.doc**. Click **Open**.

5. In the Attachments dialog box, click **OK**.

6. In the Preview pane, select the *Uses* tab. Note that the Attachments node contains an entry, as shown in Figure 8–26.

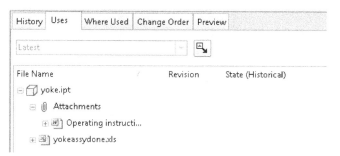

Figure 8–26

Task 4 - Rename an assembly and a part.

In this task, you will use the Rename Wizard to rename **topplate assy.iam** and **topplate.ipt**.

1. In Autodesk Vault, browse to the $*Designs\Top Plate* folder.

2. Select the two files **topplate Assy.iam** and **topplate.ipt**, right-click, and select **Rename**. The Rename Wizard opens as shown in Figure 8–27.

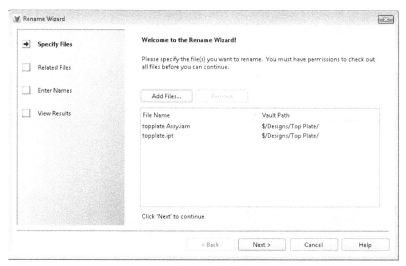

Figure 8–27

3. Click **Next>** to continue. There are no files affected by the rename so the Related Files page was automatically skipped.

4. Enter new names for each file and select the checkbox in the *Update Part Number* column for both parts, as shown in Figure 8–28.

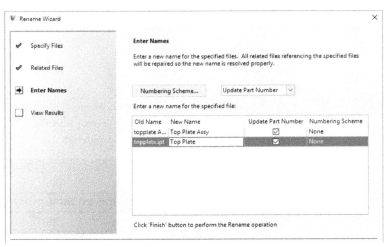

Figure 8–28

5. Click **Finish**.

6. Click **Send to Vault...** to save the report in the vault. Locate the *...\Documentation* folder and name the file **Renaming Report**. Click **Save**.

7. In the View Results page, confirm that both renames were successful, including the part number updates, as shown in Figure 8–29.

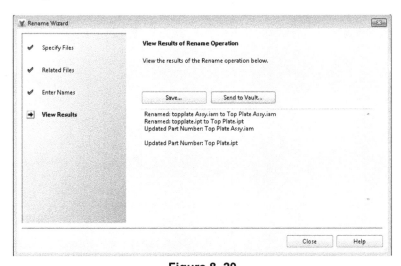

Figure 8–29

8. Click **Close**.

9. In the Main table, select **Top Plate Assy.iam**. In the Preview pane, select the *History* tab. The **Rename** operation has created Version 2 of the file and the comments have been filled in automatically, as shown in Figure 8–30.

Figure 8–30

Task 5 - Confirm Part Number Updates in iProperties.

In this task, you will add a *Part Number* column to the Main table to view and confirm that the Part Numbers have updated in the two renamed files.

1. In the Main table, select a column heading, right-click, and select **Customize View**.

2. Click **Fields...**.

3. In the Available fields list, select **Part Number** and click **Add** to add it to the list of fields to be displayed. Move it up to display after the *Name* field.

4. Click **OK** and then click **Close** to close the Customize View dialog box and view the changes. The two renamed files now display the Part Numbers of the new filenames, as shown in Figure 8–31.

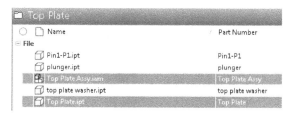

Figure 8–31

Practice 8b

Editing File Properties and Labeling

Practice Objectives

- Edit the file properties of an assembly.
- Create a label.

In this practice, you will edit file properties in the Autodesk Vault interface and create a label to mark a design milestone for the hub shaft assembly.

Task 1 - Edit the file properties of an assembly.

In this task, you will edit the file properties of an assembly and two of its parts. The file property that requires editing, **Company**, first needs to be displayed so that it can be edited.

1. Select all of the files in the $\Designs\Piston folder (**piston_assem.dwg, piston_assem.iam, piston.ipt**, and **piston_ring.ipt**) and select **Edit>Edit Properties**.

2. Click ⫿⫿ (Select Properties) to customize the list of file properties to edit.

3. Expand the Select available fields from drop-down list and select **Files**.

4. Select **Company** and click **Add** to add it to the list of file properties to edit.

5. Move **Company** so that it displays after **Author** in the list and click **OK**.

6. Double-click in the *Company* cell for **piston_assem.iam**. Enter **ABC Company** and press <Enter>. Drag the small black box in the bottom right corner of the cell to copy the value to the other *Company* cells.

7. Click **OK**.

8. The Property Edit Results window opens displaying the results with the new **Company** value, as shown in Figure 8–32.

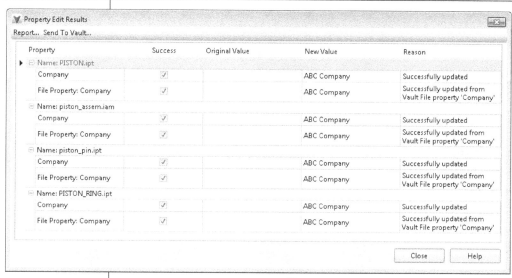

Figure 8–32

9. Select **Send To Vault** to save the report in the vault. Navigate to the *$\Documentation* folder and name the file **New Company Report**. Click **Save**.

10. Click **Close**.

Task 2 - Verify the iProperties in Autodesk Inventor and then edit them.

In this task, you will open the file **piston_assem.iam** in the Autodesk Inventor software and verify the iProperty edit. You will then edit it again in the Autodesk Inventor software.

1. In the Autodesk Inventor software, in the *Vault* tab>Access panel, click ⬛ (Open).

2. Click 🔍. In the *Search Text* field, enter **piston** and start the find.

3. In the search results window, double-click on **piston_assem.iam**.

4. Click **Open** and then click **Yes** to check out and modify the file.

5. In the Check Out dialog box, click **OK**.

6. In the Model Browser, select **piston_assem.iam**, right-click, and select **iProperties**. Select the *Summary* tab and verify that the *Company* is **ABC Company**.

7. Change the company name to **XYZ Company** and click **Apply**.

8. Click **Close** to close the iProperties window.

9. Switch to the Vault Browser. The file displays in bold blue font with an asterisk, indicating that a save is required.

10. In the Quick Access Toolbar, click 🖫 (Save).

11. Select **piston_assem.iam**, right-click, and select **Check In**.

12. Select **Close files and delete working copies**. In the *Enter comments to include* area, enter **Property changed**. Click **OK**.

13. Click **Yes** to confirm deletion of the local copy.

Task 3 - Verify the iProperty change made in Autodesk Inventor.

In this task, you will confirm that the iProperty change made in the Autodesk Inventor software reflects correctly in the Autodesk Vault software.

1. In the Autodesk Vault software, click 🔄 (Refresh) to update the Main table view in the *$\Designs\Piston* folder.

2. Select **piston_assem.iam**. In the Properties grid, note that *Company* is now **XYZ Company**.

Task 4 - Create a label.

In this task, you will create a label to mark a proposal milestone that displays the hub shaft design with a longer shaft.

1. Select **Tools>Labels**.

2. Click **New...** to create a new label.

3. The New Label dialog box opens. For the target location, click 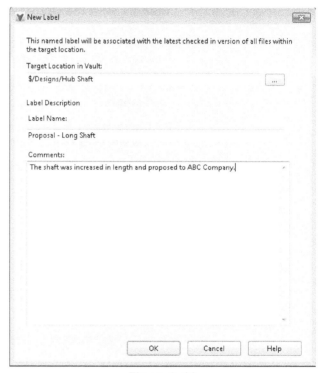 (Browse). Expand the *$\Designs* folder and select the *Hub Shaft* subfolder. Click **OK**.

4. For the label name, enter **Proposal - Long Shaft**.

5. In the *Comments* area, enter **The shaft was increased in length and proposed to ABC Company.**, as shown in Figure 8–33.

Figure 8–33

6. Click **OK**. In the Labels dialog box, the details of the new label display.

7. Click **Close** to close the Labels dialog box.

Practice 8c

Copy Design

Practice Objective

- Create a new design using the Copy Design command.

In this practice, you will make a copy of **Vise.idw** using the **Copy Design** option.

Task 1 - Start the Copy Design operation.

In this task you start the **Copy Design** command and select the files you want to copy, reuse and replace.

1. In the Main table, right-click on **Vise.idw**, and select **Copy Design**.

2. Using <Ctrl>, select files **Vise.idw**, **Vise.iam**, **Base.ipt**, and **Screw_Sub.iam**, and then right-click and select **Copy**.

3. Select **Handle_Ball.ipt**, right-click and select **Replace**. Navigate to the *Vise* folder and select **Handle_Ball-large.ipt**. The Copy Design window displays as shown in Figure 8–34.

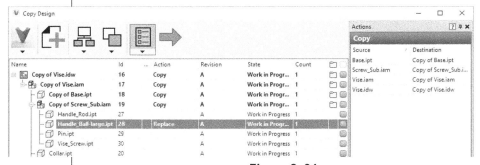

Figure 8–34

4. In the *Numbering* tab, remove the values for *Prefix*. Enter **2** in the *Postfix* column and note that the *Name* column updates as shown in Figure 8–35.

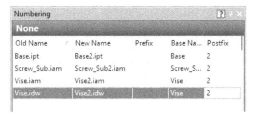

Figure 8–35

5. Click the *Folders* tab to set the folder of the copied files. Select **List View** to view the Destination Path. Click in the *Destination Path* field and then click on the ellipses button to create a new folder under *Designs* named **Vise2**. Change the Destination Path for the other copied files to *Vise2*, as shown in Figure 8–36.

Figure 8–36

Task 2 - Create a Copy of the files and view the copied files.

In this task you will create a copy of the selected files.

1. Click 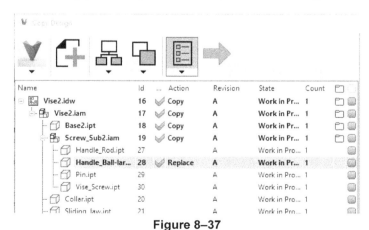 (Create Copy) on the toolbar to start the copy operation. When successful, a green checkmark will display for the **Copy** and **Replace** actions, as shown in Figure 8–37.

Figure 8–37

2. Close the Copy Design window. In the Autodesk Vault client, browse to the *Vise2* folder to view the copied files, as shown in Figure 8–38.

Figure 8–38

Task 3 - Open the Vise2 assembly.

In this task, you will open the Vise2 assembly.

1. Select **Vise2.iam**, right-click, and select **Open** to open it in the Autodesk Inventor software. Click **No** to when prompted to check out the assembly.

2. In the Vault Browser, verify that **Vise2.iam** references **Base2.ipt**, **Screw_Sub2.iam**, and **Handle_Ball-large.ipt** are under **Screw_Sub2.iam**.

Chapter Review Questions

1. When you move a file from one location to another, the file effectively remains the same in the new location and is still referenced by its children and parents.

   a. True

   b. False

2. What do you need to remember when using the **Delete** operation? (Select all that apply.)

   a. Parents need to be deleted before children.

   b. Children need to be deleted before parents.

   c. A file must be in a **Checked In** state.

   d. If a file label exists, it needs to be deleted before the file is deleted.

3. When a label has been created, which operation is used to create a package based on that label?

   a. Edit

   b. Copy Design

   c. Pack and Go

   d. Restore

4. When files are attached to other files in the vault, a link is created between the files so that they act as a single unit when they are checked out or checked in.

   a. True

   b. False

5. When using **Copy Design**, what operations can be performed on the files? (Select all that apply.)

   a. Copy

   b. Reuse

   c. Exclude

   d. Replace

Command Summary

Button	Command	Location
	Select Properties	• Property Edit dialog box

Items and Bill of Materials Management

This chapter introduces you to how to create Items and Bill of Materials (BOMs) in Autodesk Vault. You will also learn how to view, modify, and compare Bills of Materials, and differentiate between methods of creating Bill of Materials detail reports.

Learning Objectives in this Chapter

- Use the New Item, Assign/Update Item and drag and drop methods to create new items and Bill of Materials.
- Use the Bill of Materials tab to view BOMs.
- Modify Bill of Materials to add, remove, and reorder items.
- Use the Compare command to compare Bill of Materials.
- Use the Save BOM View and BOM Export commands to export a Bill of Materials to a file.
- Use the BOM Report command to create Bill of Materials reports.

9.1 Items and BOMs

Items can be created either from the Item Master or from Autodesk Inventor design files. The Item Master contains the list of all items in the Autodesk Vault. Items can be viewed from the Item Master, as shown in Figure 9–1.

Figure 9–1

Bill of Materials can be viewed when viewing an Item from the *Bill of Materials* tab, as shown in Figure 9–2.

Figure 9–2

9.2 Creating Items and BOMs

Inventor design files stored in Autodesk Vault can be assigned to items in order to create a Bill of Materials (BOM). Alternatively, items can be created first in the Item Master and then associated with design files, also known as the "BOM first" workflow.

Assign Items

How To: Assign an Item to a File

1. In Project Explorer, select one or more files, right-click and select **Assign/Update Item**, as shown in Figure 9–3.

Figure 9–3

2. The items are created in the Item Master. Select **Item Master** to view the new items, as shown in Figure 9–4.

Figure 9–4

3. To edit the item, double-click on the item to open it in its own dialog box and then click **Edit**, as shown in Figure 9–5.

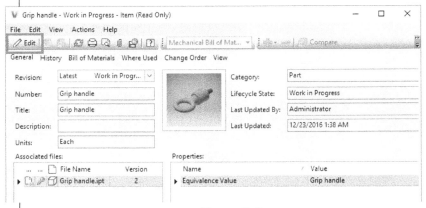

Figure 9–5

4. The item is now in edit mode, and you can make changes to it. Click **Save** to save any changes, as shown in Figure 9–6.

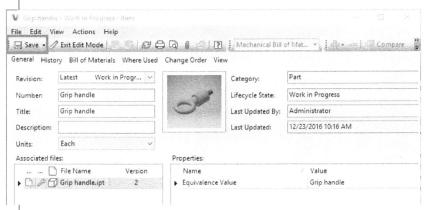

Figure 9–6

Create Items Using New Item

How To: Create Items Using the New Item Command

1. Click **Item Master.**
2. In the toolbar, click **New**, and then click **New Item,** as shown in Figure 9–7.

Figure 9–7

You can also create new items by dragging and dropping files onto the Item Master node in the browser.

3. If applicable, select a category, as shown in Figure 9–8. Click **OK**.

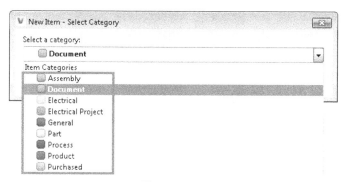

Figure 9–8

4. In the Item dialog box, in the *General* tab, enter the required values (i.e., Title, Description, Units, etc.), as shown in Figure 9–9.

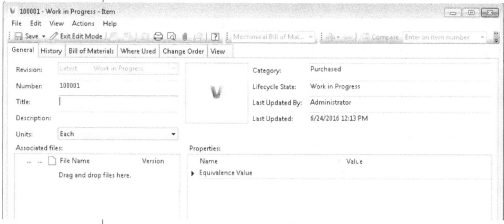

Figure 9–9

5. To add associated files and supporting documents, drag and drop the files into the *Associated files* area.

6. Click **Save and Close** when you are finished, as shown in Figure 9–10.

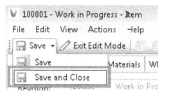

Figure 9–10

9.3 Working with BOMs

Bill of Materials management takes place in the *Bill of Materials* tab for an item.

Viewing BOMS

You can view BOMs in Autodesk Vault's Main pane by either double-clicking on an item, or through the Preview pane.

How To: View BOMs

1. Select the *Item Master* tab.
2. In the Preview pane, select the *Bill of Materials* tab to view the BOM, or double-click to open the item in a new window, as shown in Figure 9–11.

Figure 9–11

Bill of Materials (BOM) Status Icons

The BOM status icons can help you manage your BOM more effectively. These are described as follows:

Icon	Description
	Item exists in the vault.
	Item exists but the row is toggled off in the BOM.
	No item is assigned. The file is the child of a parent with an assigned item, however no item has been assigned to the child file.

	Item row consists of multiple rows that have been grouped together.
	Item row is toggled on. The item is included in all BOM processes.
	Item row is toggled off. The item is listed for tracking purposes but is not included in BOM processes.
	Item can be edited.
	Item is locked and cannot be edited.
	Item is created but has not been saved to vault yet.
	The item is obsolete. However, a newer revision may exist.
	The item is not available for editing because another user is currently editing the parent file.

Modifying BOMs

Bill of Materials modifications can include changing quantities, adding rows, deleting rows, toggling rows on or off, and reordering rows. In all cases, first click **Edit** to begin the modifications. Note that modifications can only be made when the BOM is set to a Multi-Level structure view.

How To: Change Quantity

1. Click in the *Quantity* field of an item and enter the new quantity, as shown in Figure 9–12.

Figure 9–12

How To: Add Rows

1. Right-click on the top-level item and select **Add Row>From Existing Item** or **From New Item**, as shown in Figure 9–13.

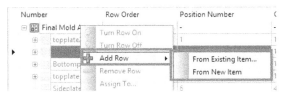

Figure 9–13

2. Follow the prompts to add a new or existing item.

How To: Delete Rows

Right-click on the top-level item and select **Remove Row**, as shown in Figure 9–14.

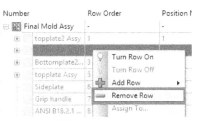

Figure 9–14

How To: Reorder Rows

To reorder rows, either:

- Change the *Row Order* column values, or
- Drag and drop the number to a different position in the same parent, as shown in Figure 9–15.

Figure 9–15

Note: Select ▦ (Restore Saved Order) in the toolbar to revert back to the last saved order.

How To: Toggle Rows On or Off

You can include items on the BOM but then hide them if you do not want them included in the BOM process.

1. In the *On/Off Row* column, click on a light bulb for an item to toggle it on or off, as shown in Figure 9–16.

Figure 9–16

2. To control the display of on and off rows, select either **All Rows**, **On Rows Only** or **Off Rows Only** from the drop-down list, as shown in Figure 9–17.

Figure 9–17

Comparing BOMs

How To: Compare Button

1. To compare the BOM of two different items, or a version of a BOM with the displayed revision, or different versions of the same item, select the items or values from the fields as shown in Figure 9–18.

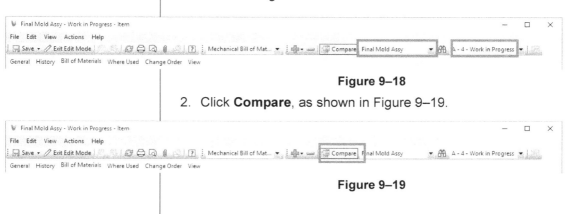

Figure 9–18

2. Click **Compare**, as shown in Figure 9–19.

Figure 9–19

3. The differences between the two BOMs are highlighted in the current BOM view, as shown in Figure 9–20.

Figure 9–20

- **Blue font:** Either the row was added or toggle on in the displayed BOM, but not in the comparison BOM or the row has an item now but was a BOM component in the comparison BOM.
- **Blue Bold font:** Values of individual properties are different.
- **Red Strikethrough:** The row does not exist, or is toggled off in the displayed BOM.

Save BOM View

How To: Save the BOM View

1. To save the view of the BOM, in the Item dialog box, in the *Bill of Materials* tab, select **File>Save BOM View**, as shown in Figure 9–21.

Figure 9–21

2. Select a destination and name for the Microsoft Excel file.

BOM Report

How To: Create a BOM Report

1. In the Item dialog box, select the *Bill of Materials* tab.
2. In the BOM Structure drop-down list, select **Multi-Level**, **First-Level,** or **Parts Only**, as shown in Figure 9–22.

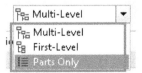

Figure 9–22

3. Right-click on any item in the list and select **BOM Report**, as shown in Figure 9–23.

Figure 9–23

4. Select a BOM template that matches the selected structure (i.e., **BOM - First-Level.rdls**, **BOM - Multi-Level.rdlc**, and **BOM - Parts-Only.rdlc**).
5. Click **OK**. The report opens in a new window.

BOM Export

How To: Export a BOM

1. In the Item dialog box, select the *Bill of Materials* tab.
2. Right-click on any item in the list and select **BOM Export**, as shown in Figure 9–24.

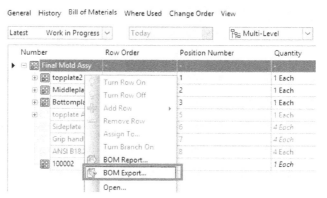

Figure 9–24

3. In the Item Export Wizard, follow the prompts to configure the report and export to a specified file format. Note that the rows that are toggled on are the only ones exported.

Practice 9a | Working with Items and BOMs

Practice Objectives

- Create an Item using Assign / Update Item.
- Modify a Bill of Materials.
- Save a Bill of Materials view.

In this practice, you will create items based on existing Autodesk Inventor files. You will then modify the BOM of the items created and export the BOM to an Excel file.

Task 1 - Create Items from Design Files using Assign / Update Item.

1. In the Main table of the Autodesk Vault client software, locate the Mold Assembly folder.

2. Use <Ctrl>+<A> to highlight all files in the folder, right-click and select **Assign/ Update Item,** as shown in Figure 9–25.

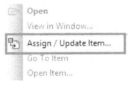

Figure 9–25

3. Click **Item Master** to view the created items.

Task 2 - Modify BOM by a Changing Quantity and Removing an Item.

1. Double-click on the item for **Final Mold Assy.iam** in the Item Master.

2. Select the *Bill of Materials* tab to view the Bill of Materials, as shown in Figure 9–26

Figure 9–26

3. Click **Edit** in the top left corner.

4. Change the quantity for the **Sideplate** and **Grip handle** from 2 to **4** as shown in Figure 9–27.

Figure 9–27

5. Right-click on **bottomplate** and select **Remove Row**.

6. Click **Yes** to confirm the removal of the row.

7. Toggle some rows on or off by clicking on the light-bulb icons in the *On/Off BOM Row* column.

8. Click **Save**.

Task 3 - Create a New Item in the BOM.

---

1. In the *Bill of Materials* tab, right-click on **Final Mold Assy**, then select **Add Row>From New Item**, as shown in Figure 9–28.

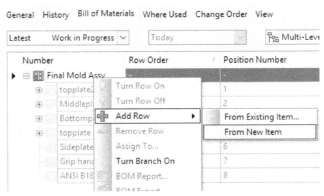

Figure 9–28

2. For the category, select **Purchased**, then click **OK**.

3. The new item is created successfully

4. Click **Save**.

Task 4 - Save a BOM View.

In this task, you will save the BOM details to an Excel file.

1. Select **File>Save BOM View.**

2. Navigate to the folder where you want to save the file and enter **Final Mold Assy BOM View** as the filename. Click **Save**, as shown in Figure 9–29.

Figure 9–29

3. Navigate to the folder where the saved file is located. Open it in Excel to view the details, as shown in Figure 9–30. Note that rows that are toggled on and off are both displayed.

Figure 9–30

4. Close the file and Microsoft Excel.

Task 5 - Compare BOM Structure Views.

In this task, you will compare the BOM Structure Views.

1. In the *Bill of Materials* tab, select **First-Level**, as shown in Figure 9–31.

Figure 9–31

2. Select **Parts Only** and **Multi-Level** to compare their results, as shown in Figure 9–32. Note that you can only modify while in the Multi-Level structure view.

Figure 9–32

3. Click **Exit Edit Mode**. Right-click on **Final Mold Assy** and select **BOM Export...**, as shown in Figure 9–33.

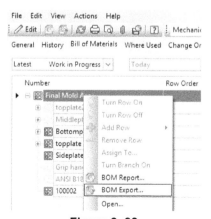

Figure 9–33

Note that only the rows that were toggled on are exported.

Chapter Review Questions

1. When items are created in the Item Master first, and then associated with design files second, it is known as the "BOM first" workflow.

   a. True

   b. False

2. In order to make changes to a Bill of Materials, what do you need to do?

   a. Toggle all rows to On.

   b. Select **First-Level** for the BOM Structure View.

   c. Click **Edit**.

   d. Reorder the BOM rows.

3. A Bill of Materials can only be edited when it is in the Multi-Level Structure View.

   a. True

   b. False

4. To save a BOM to a file that shows only the rows that are toggled On, use the _____ command.

   a. **Save BOM View**

   b. **BOM Export**

   c. **Multi-Level**

   d. **BOM Report**

Command Summary

Button	Command	Location
	Assign/Update Item	• **Shortcut:** (right-click on selected file)
	Add Row	• **Item dialog box:** Toolbar
	BOM Report	• *Bill of Materials* tab
	BOM Export	• *Bill of Materials* tab
	Compare	• **Item dialog box:** Toolbar
	New Item	• **Menu:** Actions>New Item and Standard Toolbar
	Remove Row	• **Item dialog box:** Toolbar
	Save BOM View	• **Item dialog box:** File menu

Chapter 10

Change Management

The Change Order object in Autodesk Vault enables you to manage the Change Order process of a design. In this chapter you will learn about the components of the Change Order object and how to create and approve a Change Order.

Learning Objectives in this Chapter

- Use the Add to Change Order command to create a Change Order for an item or file.
- Review and approve a Change Order.

10.1 Change Order Object Overview

The Change Order is an object in Autodesk Vault Professional that enables you to manage the changes for your design.

Select the **Change Order List** to view the interface, as shown in Figure 10–1.

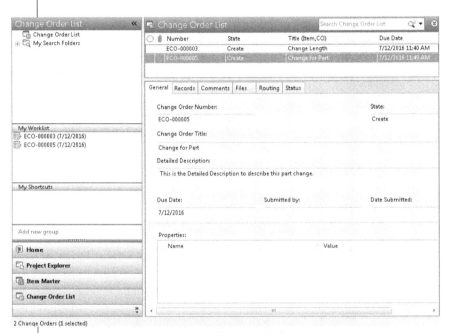

Figure 10–1

General Tab

It displays the properties of a Change Order, as shown in Figure 10–2.

Figure 10–2

Records Tab

It displays the list of files and items associated with the Change Order, as shown in Figure 10–3.

Figure 10–3

Comments Tab

It contains the details of change order decisions in the form of comments, attachments, and markups, as shown in Figure 10–4.

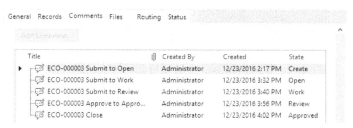

Figure 10–4

Files Tab

It lists all of the files attached to the change order. Any associated items are displayed in the *Associated Items* subtab, and the files can be viewed from the *Preview* subtab, as shown in Figure 10–5.

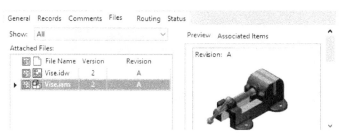

Figure 10–5

Routing Tab

It displays the routing list used to control which users are notified when a Change Order moves to a specific state, as shown in Figure 10–6.

Figure 10–6

Status Tab

It shows the current lifecycle state of the Change Order. An example is shown in Figure 10–7.

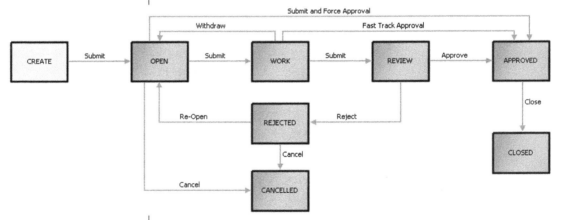

Figure 10–7

10.2 Change Order Process

The Change Order Process begins with a Change Requestor creating a Change Order. The standard roles in the Change Order process are:

- Change Requestor

- Change Administrator

- Responsible Engineer

- Reviewer

- Approver

- Notification User

Users are assigned to each of these roles. A routing list is used to control which users are assigned to each role, and when a user should be notified when a Change Order enters a certain state. The main states for a default standard Change Order are shown in Figure 10–8.

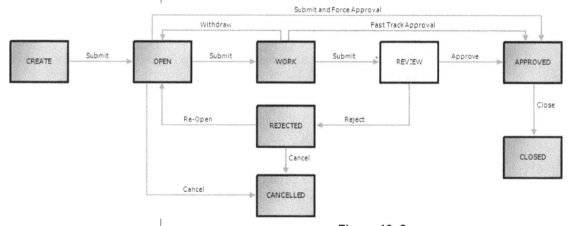

Figure 10–8

The roles and actions that occur at each stage of the Change Order Process are described below.

Create

The Change Requestor creates the change order, adds comments, attaches files, and selects the routing participants. The Change Requestor also automatically becomes a reviewer.

Open	The Change Administrator can edit the change order, if required. They can edit all values as in the Create state except the ECO number.
Work	The Responsible Engineer is notified and the Change Order Number is added to their work list. The Responsible Engineer can edit the change order and make any required changes, and then submits the change order for review.
Review	The Reviewer can view, add, and reply to comments. **Note:** Any participant can add additional Reviewers to the routing, as required.
Approved or Rejected	The Approver can review, approve, and reject a change order.
Canceled	The Change Administrator can cancel the change order or reopen a closed change order, as required.
Closed	The Notification User receives notification when the change order is closed. **Note:** If Check State is enabled, a Checker is added to the list of routing participants when a work order is rejected. The checker can review, approve, or reject the change order. A standard workflow does not include the Check State or Checker role.

Creating a Change Order

Create State (Change Requestor)

1. With a file or item selected, right-click on the file and select **Add to Change Order>To New** as shown in Figure 10–9.

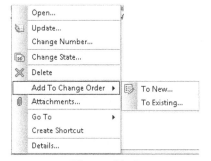

Figure 10–9

2. A window opens with the new ECO object displaying an automatically-generated Change Order Number and a State of **Create**.

3. In the *General* tab, enter a *Change Order Title* and *Detailed Description*.

4. Select the *Files* tab and attach any additional objects to the Change Order.

5. Select the *Routing* tab and click **Edit** to make any changes to the routing.

6. Select the *Status* tab and note that the next state is **Open**.

7. Select **Save** to save the ECO.

8. If no other changes are required to promote the ECO to the Open state, click 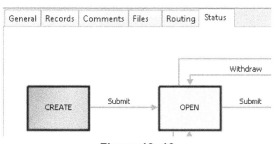 (Submit) .

9. Enter comments in the *Comment* field and click **OK**.

10. In the Main table, hold <Ctrl> and select the change order icon to go to the change order. In the *Status* tab, note that its state is **Open**, as shown in Figure 10–10.

General	Records	Comments	Files	Routing	Status

CREATE — Submit → OPEN — Submit
Withdraw

Figure 10–10

Open State (Change Administrator)

1. The Change Administrator is notified and can now edit the Change Order, if required. The Change Administrator can also determine whether the ECO should be canceled.

2. Click 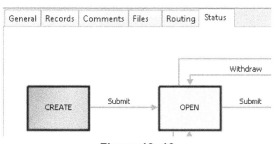 (Submit) to move the Change Order to the **Work** state, as shown in Figure 10–11.

General   Records   Comments   Files   Routing   Status

Submit and Force Appro

Withdraw   F

CREATE — Submit → OPEN — Submit → WORK — Submit

Figure 10–11

Work State (Responsible Engineer)

1. The Responsible Engineer is notified and the ECO is placed in their Worklist. If the files or items are not in the Work In Progress state yet, the Responsible Engineer will do this.
2. Make the design changes as outlined in the Change Order and check the files back into the vault. Note that the items are now listed as being updated.
3. Click ⬆ (Submit) to move the Change Order to the **Review** state, as shown in Figure 10–12

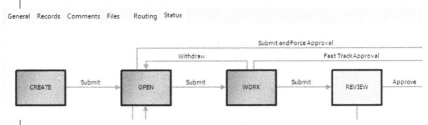

Figure 10–12

Approving a Change Order

*If **Unanimous Approval for Review State Required** is selected in the Routing Settings dialog box, all Approvers must review and submit their acceptance of the Change Order.*

Review State (Reviewers)

1. The Reviewers and Approvers are notified that there is a Change Order waiting for approval. They review files with the design changes and add their comments.

2. Click ☑ (Approve) or ☒ (Reject), as applicable, as shown in Figure 10–13.

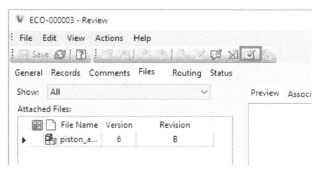

Figure 10–13

3. The Change Order moves to the **Approved** state as shown in Figure 10–14.

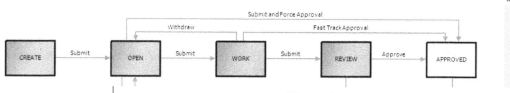

Figure 10–14

Approved State (Approvers/Change Administrator)

1. The Approver can review, approve, and reject a change order. The Change Administrator is notified. and any Work In Progress or In Review/For Review items and files on the change order are set to **Released**.

2. Click ☑ (Approve). The Change Order moves to the Closed state, as shown in Figure 10–15.

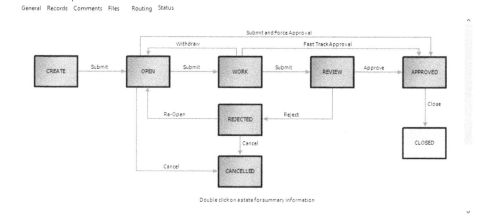

Figure 10–15

Closed State (Notification Users)

1. All Notification Users are notified.

2. In the ECO, select the Records tab and note the incremented *Revision* and *State* of the item or file as **Released**

3. If required, a Change Order Summary Report can be printed from the ECO by selecting **Actions>Print Change Order Summary**, as shown in Figure 10–16.

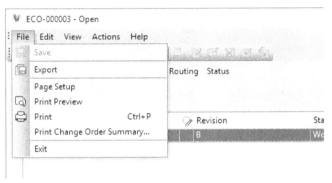

Figure 10–16

Practice 10a

Creating and Approving a Change Order Using Items

Practice Objectives

- Create a Change Order using Items.
- Approve a Change Order using Items.

In this practice, you will create, review, and approve an Engineering Change Order (ECO) using items. For instructional purposes, **user1** will have permissions to create, review, and approve a change order. Note that a company will typically have different users set up for these various roles.

Task 1 - Create an ECO (Create State: Change Requestor).

1. Log in as **user1** to the **Vault_Training** vault (no password is required for this account).

2. Locate the **Vise** item.

3. Right-click on the **Vise** item and then select **Add to Change Order>To New**, as shown in Figure 10–17.

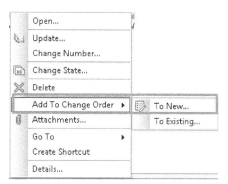

Figure 10–17

4. A window opens with the new ECO object displaying an automatically-generated *Change Order Number* and a *State* of **Create** as shown in Figure 10–18.

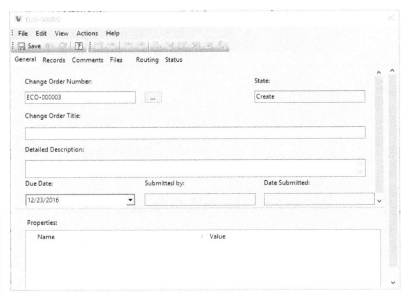

Figure 10–18

5. In the *General* tab, enter **Design Change for Piston Assembly** for the *Change Order Title* and *Detailed Description*.

6. Select the *Routing* tab to view the roles assigned to **user1**, as shown in Figure 10–19.

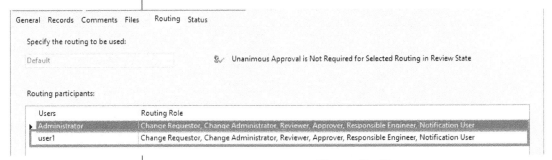

Figure 10–19

7. Select the *Status* tab to see that the current state is **Create** and the next state is **Open** as shown in Figure 10–20.

General Records Comments Files Routing Status

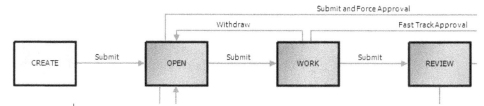

Figure 10–20

8. Select **Save** to save the ECO.

9. Select  (Submit) to promote the ECO to the **Open** state, as shown in Figure 10–21.

Figure 10–21

10. Enter comments in the *Comment* field and click **OK**.

11. In the Main table, hold <Ctrl> and select the change order icon to open the change order. Open the *Status* tab and note that the state is now **Open**, as shown in Figure 10–22.

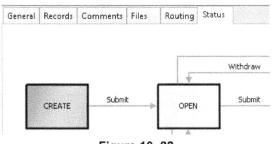

Figure 10–22

Task 2 - Edit ECO (Open state: Change Administrator)

1. The Change Administrator is now notified and can edit the ECO if required.

2. Click  (Submit) to promote the ECO to the **Work** state

Task 3 - Perform Design Work (Work state: Responsible Design Engineer)

The Responsible Engineer is notified and the ECO is placed in their Worklist. The Responsible Engineer makes the design changes as outlined in the Change Order. Once complete, they check the files back into the vault, and the items are updated.

- Click (Submit) to promote the ECO to the **Review** state

Task 4 - Review ECO (Review state: Reviewer)

The Reviewers are notified. They review the design changes as per the ECO.

- Click (Approve) to promote the ECO to the **Approved** state.

Task 5 - Approve ECO (Approved state: Approver)

The Approver can review, approve and reject a change order. The Change Administrator is notified. and any Work In Progress or In Review or For Review items and files on the change order are set to **Released**.

- Click (Close Change Order). The Change Order moves to the **Closed** state, as shown in Figure 10–23.

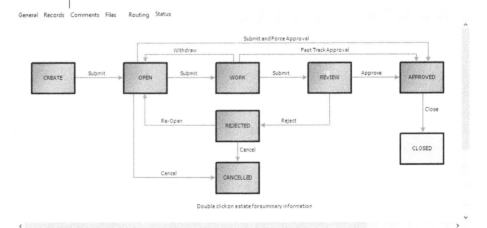

Figure 10–23

Task 6 - Close ECO (Closed State).

1. A Change State window opens. Select **Released** from the list, as shown in Figure 10–24.

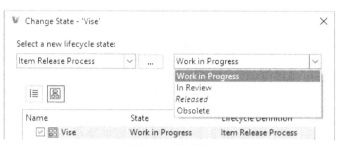

Figure 10–24

2. The Comments are entered automatically as **Released to manufacturing**. Click **OK**.

3. Select the *Records* tab of the ECO and note the incremented *Revision* and *State* of the item or file as **Released**.

4. Print a Change Order Summary Report by selecting **File> Print Change Order Summary**, as shown in Figure 10–25.

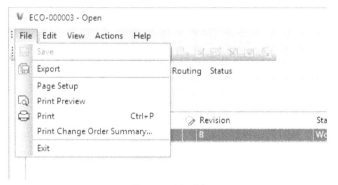

Figure 10–25

Practice 10b | Creating and Approving a Change Order Using Files

Practice Objectives

- Create a Change Order using files.
- Review, Approve and Close a Change Order using files.

In this practice, you will create, review and approve an Engineering Change Order (ECO) using files. The steps are the same as the previous practice. Again, for instructional purposes, **user1** will have permissions to create, review and approve a change order.

Task 1 - Create an ECO (Create State: Change Requestor).

1. Log in as **user1** to the **Vault_Training** vault (no password is required for this account).

2. Locate **piston_assem.iam**.

3. Right-click on **piston_assem.iam** and then select **Add to Change Order>To New**, as shown in Figure 10–26.

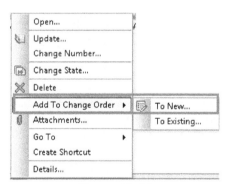

Figure 10–26

4. Edit the ECO, save it, and click (Submit) to promote to the **Open** state.

Task 2 - Edit ECO (Open state: Change Administrator)

- Edit the ECO and click 📄 (Submit) to promote to the **Work** state.

Task 3 - Perform Design Work (Work state: Responsible Design Engineer)

- Perform the design work and click 📄 (Submit) to promote to the **Review** state.

Task 4 - Review ECO (Review state: Reviewer)

- Review the ECO and click ☑ (Approve) to promote it to the **Approved** state.

Task 5 - Approve ECO (Approved state: Approver)

- Review and approve the ECO and click 📄 (Close Change Order) to promote it to the **Closed** state.

Chapter Review Questions

1. When viewing a Change Order object, what tab enables you to view which users can approve the change order?

   a. General

   b. Records

   c. Files

   d. Routing

2. While moving through the standard Change Order lifecycle states of **Create**>**Open**>**Work**>**Review**>**Approved**>**Closed**, it is at the **Work** state that the Responsible Engineer can edit the change order and make design changes.

   a. True

   b. False

3. What tab of a Change Order object is used to attach additional files to a change order?

   a. General

   b. Records

   c. Files

   d. Status

4. What does Unanimous Approval mean?

   a. Only the Administrator needs to review and submit their acceptance of the Change Order.

   b. All Approvers must review and submit their acceptance of the Change Order.

   c. Only one Approver needs to review and submit their acceptance of the Change Order.

   d. The Approved lifecycle state is skipped.

5. The Approver cannot reject a change order.

   a. True

   b. False

Command Summary

Button	Command	Location
	Approve	• **ECO dialog box:** Toolbar
	Close Change Oder	• **ECO dialog box:** Toolbar
	Reject	• **ECO dialog box:** Toolbar
	Submit	• **ECO dialog box:** Toolbar

Index

www.ingramcontent.com/pod-product-compliance
Lightning Source LLC
Chambersburg PA
CBHW080356060326
40689CB00019B/4027